Derek Coleman

A Structured Programming Approach to Data

Springer-Verlag New York

Derek Coleman
Department of Computation
Institute of Science Technology
University of Manchester
Manchester
England

Printed in the United States of America

Library of Congress Cataloging in Publication Data.
Coleman, Derek.
    A structured programming approach to data.
    Bibliography: p.
    1. Structured programming.   2. Data structures
(Computer science)   I. Title.
QA76.6.06255   001.6'42   79-11220

ISBN 0-387-91138-3 Springer-Verlag New York
9 8 7 6 5 4 3 2

Contents

Preface

Much of current programming practice is basically empirical and *ad hoc* in approach. Each problem is tackled without relation to those that have gone before; experiences are made and stored as a series of fragments. Now, under the pressure of events, this unsatisfactory state of affairs is coming to an end. Programming is becoming a technology, a theory known as *structured programming* is developing. The purpose of a theory is to categorise and explain existing practice, thus enabling it to be improved through the development of new and sharper techniques. The resulting experiences have then to be fed back into the theory so that the process of enrichment may continue. This dialectical relationship between theory and practice is essential to a healthy programming technology. The lack of such a relationship in the 1950s and 60s and the accompanying software crisis certainly confirm the converse of this proposition.

My aim in writing this book has been to explain the current state of the theory of structured programming, so that it may be used to improve the reader's practice. The book deals with two facets of programming – how to design a program in terms of abstract data structures and how to represent the data structures on real and bounded computers. The separation between program design and data structure representation leads to more reliable and flexible programs. The introduction and use of an abstract programming language as the notation for expressing both program design and the structure of data ensures, as far as is possible, that the description is machine and language independent. The reader can use the notation (or his own personal variant) for the design of structured programs whatever the actual language to be used. The ease of this task depends largely on the suitability of the language for structured programming. Some languages, such as BASIC, are clearly quite inadequate for the task owing to the paucity of their semantics. Other languages such as Pascal and its derivatives, embody in practical and tested form, the theory of structured programming. Of necessity, therefore, I have adopted a Pascal-like notation.

The book constitutes a second-level self-contained text on the role of data structuring in programming and therefore assumes a knowledge of the basic concepts of programming in a high-level language. It has evolved from the second-year undergraduate lecture course on 'Data Structures' that I have given at UMIST over the past six years. It presents as a coherent whole the ideas of Dijkstra, Hoare and Wirth on structured programming together with the earlier work of Knuth on data structures. It is hoped that the book will prove useful to all computation and computer science students doing a further course on programming, as well as to the professional programmer in commerce or industry. It is to be emphasised, however, that the ideas discussed in this book are meant to be put into use and tested in the everyday programming activity of the reader. Without interaction with practice they are dead and meaningless.

I have included four sets of exercises covering all the material in the book and have attempted to avoid questions that can be answered by direct quotation from the text. The exercises generally relate to material in more than one chapter and have been grouped accordingly. Life seldom presents us with clear-cut exercises of the form given here; it is therefore to real life that the reader should look for meaningful practice of the concepts discussed in this book.

Acknowledgements

I owe a great deal to Professor J. S. Rohl of the University of Western Australia, who first encouraged me to set my ideas down in book form. I would also like to thank Geoff King and the many other UMIST students who have contributed to this book in numerous ways. David Watt, Clive Coleman, Ronan Sleep and John Reynolds all read the draft manuscript and made many helpful comments and suggestions. I have also received much advice and assistance from my colleagues at UMIST, and for this I am extremely grateful. Special thanks go to Mrs I. Betton, Miss M. O'Brien and Mrs B. Sharples, who had the unenviable task of typing the manuscript. Finally I would like to thank Joan, Abra and Robert Coleman for all their support while this book was in preparation.

DEREK COLEMAN

1 *An Overview of Program Design*

1.1 INTRODUCTION – THE SOFTWARE CRISIS

The last decade has seen the recognition of programming as an area of study in its own right. It was only a few years ago that programming techniques could be summarised as the optimisation of loops by the removal of statements unaffected by the progress of the iteration. The concern then was largely one of efficiency. Today efficiency and optimisation are seen as secondary to the problem of reliability and correctness. Indeed Michael Jackson, an authority on program design proposes the following golden rules for optimisation.

(1) Do not do it.
(2) (This rule applies to experts only) Do not do it yet.

The radical change from program efficiency to reliability has been caused by the spiralling costs of software. A very large proportion of these costs is attributable to the propensity of program maintenance to consume very much more time and effort than would be thought reasonable or necessary. For example, a Hoskyns survey (Hoskyns, 1973) in Great Britain, which canvassed 905 installations, found that almost 40 per cent of the software effort in Great Britain goes into maintenance. That the job of maintaining a program has often proved to be so expensive is due to many reasons, mainly associated with the way the program was originally developed. The interrelated problems of program development and maintenance are so serious for the computing industry that it is no exaggeration to say that there is a software crisis.

Programs need modification if they are incorrect or if there is a change in their environment requiring a change in the function that they compute. The amount of modification can be minimised if the initial program is correct and flexible. Modification is made onerous if the program is badly designed so that it is difficult to understand. In fact, if a program is difficult to understand then it is also unlikely to be correct or flexible in the first place. A program text that is confusing is likely to be even more of a mess after modification and is never likely to prove satisfactory. The answer then is a costly rewrite from scratch.

Lack of transparency of purpose in programs can be due to a variety of reasons. Some of the more common causes of over-complexity in traditionally designed programs are as follows.

Flow of control that can be likened to a bowl of spaghetti due to a proliferation of jump instructions.
Self-modification of code making the meaning of a piece of text change dynamically at runtime.
Global flags that are set and unset in a multitude of places without explanation.
Absence of, or misleading, comment statements and other documentation.
Identifier names that do not even hint the use to which the variable or procedure is put.
Inconsistency in performing standard subtasks, for example, parameter passing to procedures.
The use of unexplained and devious tricks to optimise performance.
Programs with a monolithic or arbitrary subprogram structure.

The key to the elimination of these malpractices is to approach program design with a view to producing programs with a simple and consistent structure.

Consistency and simplicity of structure can be achieved by tackling the production of programs in a systematic and orderly fashion. Systematic design has a further advantage — it provides a defence against human error. At the end of each phase in the design of a program, the programmer can check and eliminate any errors.

The Turing machine is both simple and consistent in concept, but it could not be seriously claimed that programs written for Turing machines were easier to understand than the average opaque machine code program. Another attribute is necessary for programs to be simple to understand — they must be expressed in a way that is related to the problem they are meant to solve, not the machine on which they are to be obeyed. This is why number-crunching Algol or Fortran programs are usually easier to understand than their assembler language equivalent. It is therefore sensible to carry out program design in three phases

(1) design the algorithm
(2) design how the data associated with the algorithm are to be represented
(3) code the representation in the language to be used.

The phases are not completely independent of each other and therefore the separation can never be complete in practice. The design of the algorithm and its representation constitute what we shall call *program design*. The chief characteristic of program design is that it is often a difficult and demanding task requiring a clear head. In contrast, program coding requires only familiarity with the language or machine to be used and, in essence, is a purely mechanical task.

1.2 OBJECTIVES OF PROGRAM DESIGN

Our objective in studying program design is to consider the systematic production of programs. Ideally any design process should be able to guarantee the following.

Correctness

The program should meet its specification exactly, that is, for all possible sets of valid data the program yields the correct answers.

Flexibility

Apparently minor and reasonable changes in environment (for example, a change in VAT rate) should be accommodated without a major rewrite.

Completeness

The program should cater for all invalid or unexpected input and produce appropriate and informative error messages before irreparable damage is done. Reliance should not be placed on invalid output being detected after the run. 'Garbage in – garbage out' is not an acceptable philosophy.

Efficiency

The computation should be completed within acceptable space and time limits.

The question of efficiency needs to be placed in perspective. Of course, there is no excuse for using an inefficient algorithm as the basis of a program if a better one is known for the proposed range of input. Similarly there is no virtue in choosing an inefficient implementation of an efficient algorithm. But there is seldom reason for employing trickology which saves a few (often illusory) microseconds at the expense of program structure. In the long run the most inefficient program is the one that is incorrect, inflexible or incomplete but cannot be easily modified owing to lack of transparency. When the program works, measure it, then improve its critical sections.

Currently we do not have the techniques to be able to guarantee that our programs can meet these standards. Therefore in order to allow for human fallibility we must also make the program easy to modify by ensuring

Transparency of Purpose

The program must be simple to understand.

Program design remains, therefore, the subtle art of fashioning programs that meet all these requirements as far as possible.

1.3 THE HEART OF THE PROBLEM

Let us consider what it is about the nature of programs that makes them difficult to produce according to specification.

A program is a static piece of text which, when executed by a processor on a particular data value, produces a computation. In general there is a different computation for each possible data value. Every program can therefore evoke an infinite (or extremely large) set of computations. In writing a finite piece of program text we are trying to control an infinite set of computations. The problem is thus one of dealing with the unmastered complexity of an infinite set. The traditional mathematical/scientific approach when dealing with such unmanageable problems is to structure them into more manageable subproblems. To design more reliable programs we must use the maxim of divide and rule, that is, break the program into more manageable subprograms or *modules*. The program text should be structured so that the set of computations it can evoke is structured and then amenable to reason.

1.4 STEPWISE REFINEMENT (Wirth, 1971)

The advantages of breaking a problem into subproblems are that it allows us

(1) to concentrate on the (hopefully) easier solution to the smaller more manageable subproblem
(2) to reason more easily about the solution to the problem itself.

There is, of course, a major proviso that we break the problem into 'sensible' subproblems, that is, subproblems must be independent of each other so that we can tackle them independently. How to find sensible subproblems is to a large extent dependent on experience of problem-solving. The process of problem-solving involves travelling along a path from what is to be solved (the problem) until we arrive at how it can be solved (the solution). If the journey is made in steps which are small enough to check, we can be sure that the final solution does indeed solve the original problem. We can keep each step small by postulating solution to each problem as a series of solutions to a small number of subproblems. Each step is essentially, therefore, a small refinement of what is to be done in terms of how it can be done. This process is known as *stepwise refinement*; it is discussed more fully in chapter 5 and is fundamental to the approach of the entire book.

1.5 WHAT DO WE MEAN WHEN WE SAY A PROGRAM 'WORKS'?

A program that 'works' is one that contains no errors or, in other words, is correct. It happens that a user of a program and the programmer may have quite different interpretations and expectations of a correct program. Consider the following possible interpretations of correctness.

(1) The program compiles without syntax errors.
(2) The program gives the right results for a small number of sets of data.
(3) The program gives the right results for deliberately awkward or difficult sets of data.
(4) The program gives the right results for all possible sets of valid data.

Obviously the user would like his program to be totally correct (level 4). The inexpert programmer will be satisfied when he reaches level 2. The programmer's dilemma is that level 3 is the highest that can be achieved by purely empirical means — by running the program on test cases. No matter how many tests the program may have passed successfully, just one set of data on which it fails is enough to show that it is not totally correct. A plausible assertion that the program is totally correct requires a full understanding of why it works together with the careful design of test cases. An understanding of why a program works can best be gained during the design process, for the heart of stepwise refinement is to break a problem P into subproblems $P_1, P_2, P_3, \ldots$, and showing that the solutions of $P_1, P_2, P_3, \ldots$, taken together constitute a solution to P. Indeed if we cannot construct this argument at each stage of the design process then we have no rational grounds for faith in our product — the program.

1.6 SUMMARY

1. Programs should be

(a) correct
(b) flexible
(c) complete
(d) efficient
(e) transparent of purpose.

2. These are objectives best achieved by using a systematic design method that produces programs expressed in a simple consistent and problem-orientated manner.
3. Programming is difficult because we are dealing with the problem of the unmastered complexity of an infinite set.
4. The process of decomposing problems into subproblems by concentrating on similarities and temporarily ignoring differences is known as the process of stepwise refinement.
5. A correct program yields correct answers for all possible sets of valid data.

1.7 BIBLIOGRAPHICAL NOTES

The software crisis and program design are discussed in depth in the books *Practical Strategies for Developing Large Software Systems* (Horowitz, 1975), *Software Engineering* (Naur and Randell, 1969), *Program Test Methods* (Hetzel, 1973) and also in *Techniques of Program Structure and Design* (Yourdon, 1975). The method of stepwise refinement was introduced by Wirth in his paper of that name (Wirth, 1971); it is also dealt with in his two books (Wirth, 1973 and 1975) as well as chapter 5 of this book.

A brief but excellent introduction to the main areas of structured programming is given in Gries (1974).

2 *Program Design Notation*

2.1 AN ABSTRACT PROGRAMMING LANGUAGE

In this chapter we introduce a vehicle for expressing the structure and content of programs as we design them using the process of stepwise refinement. The notation for doing this may be called an *abstract programming language* because programs written in the notation are not intended to be run directly on a computer, they have to be coded into a real programming language. An abstract programming language performs the same role that in earlier times flowcharting was supposed to do; it is an informal notation to be used *during* program design. The abstract language used here is an informal extension of the language Pascal. It should be easily readable by anyone familiar with Pascal or any other Algol-like language. The notation is of necessity informal and is introduced by explaining features as and when they occur in the exposition. The essence of structure is organisation. The two dynamically related parts of a program — flow of control and accessing of data — must be organised in a simple and consistent manner. The structuring concepts applicable to each are considered in turn.

2.2 STRUCTURING CONTROL

There are two aspects to the structuring of the flow of control through programs — the modular building blocks representing actions and a program schemata for their interconnection.

2.2.1 Modules

The obvious and sensible choice for building blocks is the subprogram units available in all Algol-like languages — statements, procedures, and functions (type procedures).

A *statement* is any operation that may be considered indivisible at the current stage of the design. We need to be free to use any suitable notation for specifying operations. The only requirement is that the statement should describe, as precisely as possible, what action is required.

Depending on the circumstances, all of the following may be considered statements

"read and process all the input"
"x = −b + sqrt (b ↑ 2 − 4 ∗ a ∗ c)"
"print ("data − error")"

During the design process we may realise that the program requires the same action to operate on different values at different places or times. This is accommodated by the familiar programming language concept of specifying a procedure or subroutine with parameters. We denote the calls or uses of such procedures by the procedure name followed by the parameter information, if any, in brackets. When we are able to give the definition of procedures in terms of more elementary statements we shall specify these by use of a *procedure.*

For example, if we want to be able to print a varying number of blank lines we may postulate a procedure 'print blank lines (*n*)' where the value of *n* is an integer determining the number of such lines. A call of this procedure to print five blank lines would be the statement

    print blank lines (5)

The definition of the procedure would be

    procedure print blank lines (*n* : integer);
    begin
    repeat n times
        print one blank line
    end

A function is a procedure which returns a value to the procedure name, enabling it to be used in an expression. The definition of a function sqrt would have the heading

    function sqrt (*x* : real) : real

indicating that sqrt requires one real formal parameter *x* and returns a real value associated with the name sqrt. A function is used in the context of an expression, for example, *y* := 3.0 ∗ sqrt (2). When defining procedures it is necessary to specify which, if any, of the parameters are input−output parameters (that is, ones that may be altered during the execution of the procedure). This is indicated by writing **var** in front of the parameter(s) concerned. Thus the heading

    procedure divide (*x,y*: integer, **var** remainder, quotient: integer)

introduces a procedure with four integer valued parameters

    x ⎫ which are input parameters and not modified by the
    y ⎭ execution of divide

and

    remainder ⎫ which are input−output parameters and may be
    quotient   ⎭ changed by the execution of divide

Any assignment within a procedure or function body to a parameter, other than a **var** parameter, does not affect the value of the actual parameter outside the scope of the procedure body. It must be stressed that the procedure concept is fundamental for program structuring, and that it is often desirable to formulate an action as a procedure (or function) even when it occurs only once and the usual motive of shortening text is absent.

Program clarity can be enhanced because a procedure is self-contained and the procedure heading provides a convenient place to convey information about the interface with the calling module. The interface between modules may be thought of as a contract regarding the state of the computation. A module 'contracts' to bring about a certain result state provided the calling module ensures that the input state satisfies the necessary input condition.

2.2.2 Program Schemata

It is clear that the interconnection of statements or procedures should be

(1) simple so as to facilitate transparency and correctness
(2) powerful enough to be able to compute the same function as a program
      written using an unrestricted schemata.

A further requirement on any schemata is suggested by the nature of statements and procedures. Each module represents a single operation and has a single entry and exit point. It is desirable that this property be preserved when

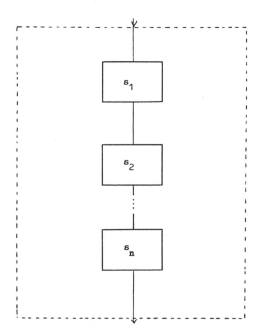

Figure 2.1 Flowchart of a sequence of statements

we interconnect a group of modules to form a 'larger' operation. The single entry/exit point restriction allows for a simple interface between modules at all levels in the program. Program clarity can be aided by the explicit definition of the interface contract using informative comment statements.

The simplest interconnection is that of *sequencing*; a sequence of modules is equivalent to a time-succession of the individual computations that they evoke.

This structure is represented by an Algol-like compound statement

> **begin**
> s_1;
> s_2;
> .
> .
> .
> s_n;
> **end**

its flowchart equivalent is shown in figure 2.1.

Examples

(i)   **begin**
     read(n);
     print(n);
     process(n);
     print(result)
   end

(ii)   **begin**
     $t := a$;
     $a := b$;
     $b := c$;
     $c := t$;
   end

Alternation is a more complex interconnection allowing the execution of a statement to be under the control of a condition

> **if** ? **then** s_1 or   **if** ? **then** s_1 **else** s_2

In some circumstances a generalised alternative statement known as a **case** statement is useful. A **case** statement provides a choice between more than two possibilities. The flowchart equivalents of the three alternation constructs are shown in figures 2.2, 2.3 and 2.4. Alternation permits computations to be specified as a choice or selection of a set of computations.

Examples

(i)   **if** $m < u$ **then** process(m)
(ii)   **if** $m < u$ **then** process(m) **else** process(u)
(iii)   **case** i **of**
     1 : process1;
     2 : process2;
     3 : process3
   end

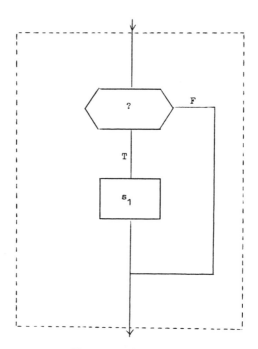

Figure 2.2 **if** ? **then** s_1

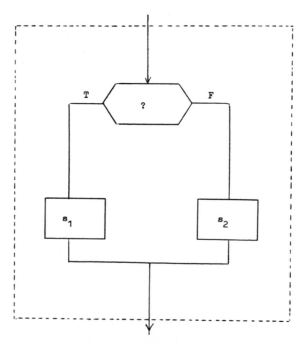

Figure 2.3 **if** ? **then** s_1 **else** s_2

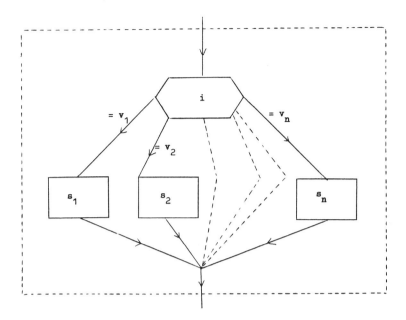

Figure 2.4 **case** i **of**

$$v_1 : s_1;$$
$$v_2 : s_2;$$
$$v_n : s_n$$
end

which is shorthand for the sequence

```
begin
if i = 1 then process1
else if i = 2 then process2
else if i = 3 then process3
else error
end
```

Sequencing and alternation by themselves are not powerful enough to allow the specification of computations that can be decomposed into a varying number of subcomputations. For this we need *repetition* or iteration constructs.

The two basic repetitive constructs are **while** condition **do** s, and **repeat** s **until** condition. The flowchart forms of these loops are shown in figures 2.5 and 2.6.

They allow us to specify computations of the form 'do a sufficient number' of a certain subcomputation. In the case of the **while** loop the statement s is executed zero or more times and the iteration terminates when the condition ? becomes false. The **repeat** loop executes s one or more times and the iteration

12

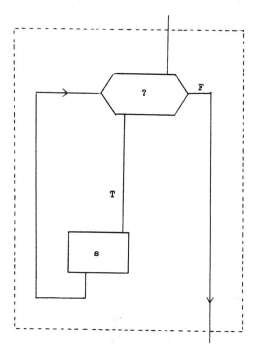

Figure 2.5 **while** ? **do** *s*

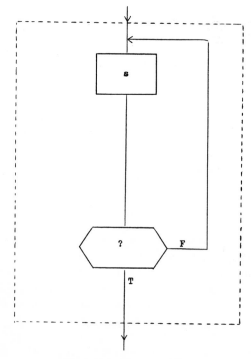

Figure 2.6 **repeat** *s* **until** ?

terminates when the condition ? becomes true. In fact the **repeat** *s* **until** ? construct is strictly redundant since

    repeat *s* **until** ?

can be replaced by

    begin
    s;
    while not ? **do**
        s
    end

The various **for** statements with controlled variables are merely special cases of these statements.

Examples

  (i)   **while** $x > y$ **do**
          $x := x - z$
  (ii) **repeat**
          read (record)
      until end-of-file
  (iii) **begin**
      read (record);
      while not (end-of-file)
          do read (record)
      end

    Any piece of text formed from these statements or procedure calls using the sequencing, alternation and repetition constructs, constitutes a *compound statement* and may be used as a statement in any of these constructs. Statements may be nested to any depth.

Example

    print (*n*), process (*n*), read (*n*),
    print (results), and
    print ('end of program')

are all statements so we may use them to construct

    begin
    read(*n*);

```
while n ≥ 0
    do begin
        print(n);
        process(n);
        print (results);
        read(n)
    end;
print ('end-of-program')
end
```

The program schemata composed of *sequencing, alternation* and *repetition* is certainly simple and well understood. The only significant interconnection that we have omitted is the **goto**. The reason for its omission is that use of the **goto** almost invites violation of the single entry/exit point condition. In the words of Wirth 'the **goto** statement allows the instantaneous invention of any form of composition which is the key to any kind of structural irregularity'.

The schemata can be proved to be as powerful as any other, yet there are some situations where we can only avoid the use of the **goto** with the penalty of inefficiency or inelegance of style; these situations usually occur when trying to remove **goto**s from an existing program. The point is that the absence of jumps is not the prime aim of structuring control but the final outcome of the exercise. We are concerned with methods for designing programs which can be easily modified, not with modifying existing programs.

An important aspect of design is the transparency of purpose of the program text; consequently it is desirable to include non-executable *comment* statements in our abstract programs. These comments should be used to specify *what* is being computed — it is the job of the executable statements to specify *how* it is being computed. Sometimes what is being computed is best expressed by making explicit the relationships which hold between the values of the variable at a particular point in the program. Throughout this book comments are denoted by including them in braces { }.

Examples

(i)   **begin**
       {interchange the values of a and b}
       $t := a$;
       $a := b$;
       $b := t$
       end

(ii)   **begin**
       $\{n \geq 0\}$
       $i = n$;
       $p = 1$;
       while $i > 0$ **do begin**

$$p := 2 * p;$$
$$i := i - 1$$
end
$$\{n \geqslant 0 \text{ and } p = 2 \uparrow n\}$$
end

2.3 STRUCTURING DATA

To structure a program into meaningful procedures we must also structure the data into meaningful and significant items; and in a high-level language the significance of an item of data is expressed in the type to which it belongs.

It is common to many languages that the programmer has to specify the type of every variable, either explicitly on declaration or implicitly through the choice of identifier. By specifying the *type* of a variable the programmer defines the set of values that can be assumed by the variable. Thus an Algol 60 boolean variable can only assume the values *true*, and *false*. Similarly the declaration

integer x

states that x can assume only integral numerical values. It should be noted that although we often pretend otherwise, integer variables take on only a subset of the integers, the actual subset being determined by the implementor in accordance with the design of the computer hardware.

One of the main advantages of high-level languages over assembly languages is that the former provide types that correspond to the concepts of their particular application area. Thus whereas an assembly language program has to manipulate items of data at the bit-pattern level, an Algol or Fortran program manipulates atomic items of data such as integers or reals. This considerably simplifies the task for the high-level language programmer, for he is freed from worrying about the details of the implementation of integers or reals on whatever computer he happens to be using.

Associated with each type there is a set of meaningful operations built into the programming language. The set of operations is permissive rather than restrictive; the programmer is always free to extend the set by writing procedures and building a library of such routines. Not all concepts in numerical mathematics are conveniently represented by the simple types integers, reals and booleans; most languages provide arrays so as to permit processing of vectors, matrices and tables. The relationship between these concepts and arrays is obvious. In mathematics a set of related variables $x_1, x_2, \ldots, x_n$ is known as a vector $\mathbf{x}$; in Algol 60 the declaration **array** $x[1 : n]$ creates the set of related variables $x[1], x[2], \ldots, x[n]$. The Algol facilities for accessing array elements mirror those of mathematics.

Programming languages do not usually provide built-in array operations such as array multiplication, but the user can write his own procedures for this purpose. Arrays are a structured type because an array value is composed of (more primitive) values such as reals, integers or booleans.

Arrays are central to any account of data structures. Many of the principal languages used for general-purpose programming have them as their only explicitly allowable structure. This has come about because arrays can be used in many problem areas, they are easily implemented (main store is an array of word values) and they are simple to understand. All these reasons have led to a situation where, for some, all structured data is seen directly in terms of arrays. This usually results in programs that have poor structure because they are expressed in terms that are relevant to the storage organisation, rather than the concepts of the problem area.

The need for other more complex data structures can best be illustrated by considering the use of computers for non-numerical applications. The concepts of these areas are different from those of numerical mathematics. A text-handling program, for example, will require a representation for strings. We may regard a character string as simply an array of characters and therefore use arrays to represent strings. Such a representation often has a number of disadvantages arising from the nature of string processing itself. An essential characteristic of strings is their variable length. During the course of execution of a string-handling program, string variables will hold values of varying length. The storage requirements of this representation may well become excessive owing to the fragmentation of store into used and unused portions of differing lengths. The only solution to this problem is the frequent compaction of store with the consequent time overhead. The choice of an inappropriate data structure causes storage management problems due to the different characteristics of string processing and vector handling. In chapter 9 we shall deal with the efficient representation of strings and similar dynamic structures.

2.4 WHAT IS A DATA STRUCTURE?

A type determines the class of values that may be assumed by a variable or expression. A *structured type* is a type defined in terms of other types. Associated with a type there must be a set of operations on values of that type. Some of these operations can usually be considered to be more primitive than others because they can be used as building blocks to construct other operations. An important part of the design of structured programs is to isolate the concepts in the problem and to specify corresponding types together with relevant primitive operations. The choice of operations should be determined by the application, though where convenient they should be logically complete to allow reusability.

We define a *data structure* as a *structured type together with some operations on that type*. This definition differs from common usage in that it gives explicit mention of the operations on the type. This is reasonable because

(1) in any particular problem we cannot conceive of a type without the operations on it

(2) nor can we implement a type without knowing what operations are to be performed on it.

For example, we cannot isolate integers from the arithmetic operations on them, nor can we conceive of buffers without operations for adding and removing items.

An important aspect of this book is to consider the data structures that are commonly found useful, and the methods of implementing them.

2.5 UNSTRUCTURED DATA TYPES

All structured data must, in the last analysis, be composed of unstructured components belonging to an unstructured type. The definitions of some of these unstructured types (for example, reals, booleans and integers) are usually determined by the implementation language. Theoretically reals and integers are sufficient for all purposes. It is sensible, however, to allow a programmer to define his own types, both to make explicit the significance of a variable and the values it may assume and to permit the subsequent design of an efficient implementation.

In particular a device often used by many programmers† is to use an integer not as a numeric quantity as such, but to represent a particular choice from a small number of alternatives. The full list of alternatives and the corresponding integral values is usually included in the program comments or documentation. From our viewpoint such a quantity should be regarded not as an integer but rather as of some new type. To specify new types in our notation requires a **type** definition.

        type vacation = (long, xmas, easter)
        type transaction = (sales, loss, return, purchase, other)

The first example defines that a variable of the type vacation can only assume a value from the set of values {long, xmas, easter}. Further, this set is the set of all constants of the type vacation. From the second example we see that the set of values (and constants) of the type transaction is {sales, loss, return, purchase, other}. Types defined in this way are said to be *declared by enumeration.* An important restriction is that a constant should only appear in a single enumerative type declaration; in this way we can always avoid ambiguity.

To declare a variable of a particular type we use a **var** declaration, of form

        var <identifier>   :   <type>

for example

        var nextvac   :   vacation;
        document   :   transaction;
        x, y, z   :   integer

† Of course. in Algol 60, Fortran or Cobol, he has no choice.

The first **var** declaration creates a variable nextvac of type vacation. The last declaration creates three variables *x*, *y* and *z* of type integer.

We may also specify the type of a variable implicitly without giving the type a name. Thus the variable slowiodevice may either be a cardreader, lineprinter, tapereader, or a terminal.

> **var** slowiodevice : (cardreader, lineprinter, tapereader, terminal)

In our notation we have adopted some features of the Pascal block structure and consequently all declarations appear at the start of a block and are valid only within the scope of the block. We must also define a type before any variables of that type are declared. For example

```
program example;
type vacation = (long, xmas, easter);
     transaction  = (sales, loss, return, purchase, other);
var nextvac    :  vacation;
    document    :  transaction;
begin
nextvac         := xmas;
   .
   .
   .
end
```

is valid but

```
program example;
type transaction = (sales, loss, return, purchase, other);
var nextvac       :  vacation;
    document       :  transaction;
begin
nextvac              := xmas;
   .
   .
   .
end
```

is invalid because the type definition vacation is missing. The scope rules of the notation are generally in keeping with the spirit of Algol-like languages.

It is sometimes convenient to regard the set of values of an enumeration type to be ordered, in the order of the enumeration. Thus only the enumeration

> **type** dayofweek = (sunday, monday, tuesday, wednesday, thursday, friday, saturday)

corresponds correctly to the first day of the week being sunday which is followed by monday, etc.

We may also specify a type as a subrange of an ordered type

type weekday = (monday .. friday)
type ageofchild = (0 .. 14)

In the first example a variable of type weekday may assume values monday, tuesday, wednesday, thursday and friday; in the second variable of type ageofchild may assume any non-negative integer less than 15.

Subrange types are a matter of controversy and often it is better to specify variables as belonging to the full range and indicate the meaningful range by a comment statement at the point of declaration.

We need only a few basic operations for the manipulation of unstructured types. These are essentially an extension of the normal facilities for handling integers and reals and have an intuitively obvious meaning.

(a) assignment

trumps := heart
nextvac := xmas;

(b) test for equality or inequality

if trumps = heart **then** . . .;
if today $<$ payday **then** . . .;

where the comparison is between variables of the same type.

2.6 IMPLEMENTATION OF UNSTRUCTURED TYPES

There are no problems regarding the implementation of an enumeration type. Simply map the values of the type T in stated order on to integers in the range 0 to $n - 1$, where n is the cardinality of the type. The usual representation of a subrange is obtained by giving each value the same representation that it had in the original type. A check should be made to ensure that the value is within the specified range.

When implementing a type it is necessary to decide on an initial preset value of every variable on declaration. In the absence of any guidance from the problem area, the zero or null value should be chosen.

2.7 SUMMARY

1. An abstract programming language is a notation for expressing program design.
2. The three basic control structures are sequencing, alternation and repetition. The **goto** is omitted because it is an invitation to make a bowl of spaghetti out of the flow of control.

3. The type of a variable is the set of values that may be assumed by the variable. A structured type is one defined in terms of other types.

4. Data structure = structured type + operations.

5. Basic unstructured types are either built-in like integers or declared by enumeration, for example

    type season = (winter, spring, summer, autumn)

2.8 BIBLIOGRAPHICAL NOTES

The abstract programming language used throughout this book is based on Pascal (Jensen and Wirth, 1975) and is essentially a development of the notation used in Hoare (1972b).

    Structuring the flow of program control originates from the Dijkstra (1968) letter 'Goto statement considered harmful'. Though the idea of avoiding the use of **goto**s was fairly well known by the mid 60s (for example, Landin, 1966). Peterson *et al.* (1973) show that **goto**s can be eliminated without loss of generality. The December 1974 issue of *Computing Surveys* was devoted to structured programming and includes an excellent article on the use of **goto**s in structured programming by Knuth (1974), as well as Wirth (1974).

3 *Arrays*

3.1 ARRAY STRUCTURES

Array structures are the most common form of data structure and are familiar to most programmers. Arrays in programming languages originated from the mathematical concept. In mathematics a set of related variables $a_1, a_2, \ldots, a_n$ is referred to as the vector **a**, in programming such a structure is known as an **array** and would be declared in Algol as **array** $a[1:n]$.

Elements of an array are all of the same type and may be individually selected by the use of subscripts. The idea of an array extends easily to sets of variables with two subscripts so providing an analogue of the matrix. For example, the set of variables

$$a = \{a_{ij} | i = 1, 2, \ldots, m \text{ and } j = 1, 2, \ldots, n\}$$

declared in Algol by **array** $a[1:m, 1:n]$, is a two-dimensional array.

Any number of subscripts or *dimensions* can be allowed to define array structures, but many programming languages provide for only one, two or three dimensions.

The use of arrays is not restricted to mathematical applications. For instance, a directory with a fixed number of entries may be regarded as a one-dimensional array of entries $e_1, e_2, \ldots, e_n$. Indeed, any sequence with a fixed number of components may be regarded and implemented as a one-dimensional array.

The use of the word dimension to characterise the number of array subscripts also highlights the spatial relationship between array elements. n-dimensional arrays may be used to represent values in a discrete n-dimensional space. In particular two-dimensional arrays are frequently used to represent information which needs to be manipulated or output in tabular form, for example, stock-level reports, mathematical tables, or boards in game-playing programs.

An array of n dimensions may be regarded as a one-dimensional array of elements which are arrays of $n-1$ dimensions, for example, the two-dimensional array $a = \{a_{ij} | i = 1, w, \ldots, m \text{ and } j = 1, 2, \ldots, m\}$ may be considered as the one-dimensional array $\{a_i | i = 1, 2, \ldots, m\}$ each of whose elements, a_i, is a one-dimensional array $a_i = \{a_{ij} | j = 1, 2, \ldots, n\}$.

In general, an **array** structured value may be defined as a fixed sized, finite, set of values known as elements; each element is of the same type and may be individually referenced by the use of subscripts. The number of *dimensions* of an array is the number of subscript values required to reference an array element. The array type is the type of its elements.

3.2 ARRAYS AND FUNCTIONS

Arrays are particularly important in programming because of their relationship to functions and mappings.

Programming is essentially using computers to evaluate functions. A function $F : D \to R$, tells us how the elements of one set, the domain D, may be transformed into the elements of another, the range R. (See figure 3.1.)

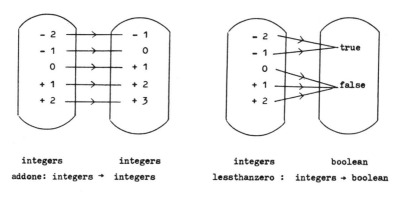

```
    integers        integers           integers           boolean
  addone: integers → integers       lessthanzero :   integers → boolean
```

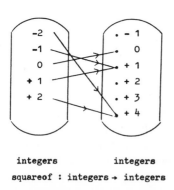

```
    integers        integers
  squareof : integers → integers
```

Figure 3.1 Diagrammatic representation of some functions

Consider the function squareof, it is normally specified by an algorithm; however, if its domain is made finite (for example, if we restrict it to positive integers less than 100) we could equally well specify squareof by a linear table of range values, the value of squareof(i) occurring in the position corresponding to a_i. (See figure 3.2.)

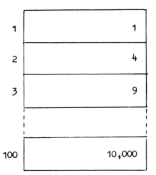

Figure 3.2 The function squareof [i: 1 .. 100] .. 1 .. 10000

From the viewpoint of evaluation, all functions have a finite domain because we can only require a finite portion of the function in a finite amount of time. Therefore, in choosing a computer representation for a function we may either produce a program from the algorithm or, if we have prior knowledge of domain range pairs we may store the function as an array structure, each domain value being a subscript and its element being the corresponding domain value.

Array structures are therefore a structural or static representation of functions. Pascal uses a notation for arrays that makes clear this relationship

m : **array** D **of** R

which declares m to be an array that maps values of type D into values of type R. Using this notation Algol declarations such as

integer squareof [1 : 100]
real array x [4 : 15]
boolean array z [2 : 10]

are written as

squareof: **array** [1 .. 100] **of** integer
x: **array** [4 .. 15] **of** real
z: **array** [2 .. 10] **of** boolean

(The declaration of an array fixes the domain and range types and the array size;† the size of an array is constant throughout its lifetime) The declaration does not specify the function itself, in fact since array elements may be updated the function being represented may change during the lifetime of the array.

In most programming languages, arrays are restricted to mappings from integers to integers, reals or booleans. This is an arbitrary restriction, any sufficiently small finite type may be used as domain and any type as range. For example, in a payroll program the number of hours worked on each day of the week by a worker could be stored in an array

hoursworked: **array** dayofweek **of** real

† Number of elements.

A value of this type might be

> sunday : 0.0
> monday : 10.0
> tuesday : 9.0
> wednesday : 11.0
> thursday : 8.5
> friday : 8.5
> saturday : 3.0

and therefore hoursworked[tuesday] = 9.0, hoursworked[saturday] = 3.0, etc.

3.3 IMPLEMENTATION OF ARRAYS

The implementation of one-dimensional arrays in store is familiar to most programmers. The usual implementation allocates one or more whole words to each element of the array. The memory address of each element is easily computed: first, the value of the subscript is converted to its integer representation; then this is multiplied by the number of words occupied by each element; and finally the result is added to the address of the first element of the array. The normal addressing mechanism of the computer can be used to access and update this value independently of the other elements of the array.

n-dimensional arrays ($n \geqslant 2$) are stored as if they were arrays of arrays, many compilers store two-dimensional arrays as an array of rows (rather than an array of columns). Consider the array declaration

> b: **array** $[1 .. 3, 3 .. 5]$ **of** real

the elements would normally be stored in row-by-row order

$$b[1,3], b[1,4], b[1,5], b[2,3], b[2,4], b[2,5], b[3,3], b[3,4], b[3,5]$$

The problem is to evaluate the position of a particular element from its subscripts.

This is essentially the primary school problem of converting mixed base numbers such as days, hours and minutes, into minutes, or years, months, weeks and days into days. For example, the relative location of some element $b[d,h,m]$ in

> **array** $[0 .. 6, 0 .. 23, 0 .. 59]$ **of** integer

is equal to the number of minutes in d days, h hours m minutes for values less than 1 week, that is, $b[d,h,m]$ is stored as element $d * 24 * 60 + h * 60 + m$ relative to the base.

Consider the general array declaration

> b: **array** $[i_1 .. j_1, i_2 .. j_2, ..., i_n .. j_n]$ **of** integer

an expression for the relative location of any element can be obtained as follows.

From the array declaration the range of each subscript p_r, can be evaluated

$$p_r = j_r - i_r + 1$$

By considering the simple example mentioned above it can be seen that the elements of b, $b[k_1, k_2, \ldots, k_n]$, are stored as follows. Elements with successive

k_n values are stored at addresses differing by 1
k_{n-1} values are stored at addresses differing by p_n
k_{n-2} values are stored at addresses differing by $p_n \cdot p_{n-1}$

and in general, elements with successive

k_r values are stored at addresses differing by $p_n \cdot p_{n-1} \ldots p_{r+1}$

$$= \prod_{m=r+1}^{n} p_m$$

In general, therefore, the element $b[k_1, k_2, \ldots, k_n]$ will be stored at the address

$$(k_1 - i_1) \prod_{m=2}^{n} p_m + (k_2 - i_2) \prod_{m=3}^{n} p_m + \cdots + (k_{n-1} - i_{n-1}).p_n + (k_n - i_n)$$

beyond the bases address of the array.

This expression may be factorised as

$$(((((k_1 - i_1) \cdot p_2 + (k_2 - i_2)) \cdot p_3 + (k_3 - i_3)) \cdot p_4 + \ldots) \ldots)p_n + k_n - i_n)$$

The factorised expression is preferable, since it requires only $n - 1$ multiplications and additions to evaluate the address of an element relative to its base address. The function for evaluating the location of an array element relative to its base is known as the *mapping* function.

The mapping function method of storage can be inefficient if references to the elements of the array are frequent and if multiplication time is long, so that the work calculating the address of the elements is significant. An alternative method is to store some of the structure information with the structure itself. This is sometimes known as the tree or descriptor method. The essence of the method is to store an n-dimensional as a one-dimensional array of 'rows' where each 'row' is an $n - 1$ dimensional array stored in the same manner. Each element of the one-dimensional arrays contains the base address of the 'row' to which it corresponds. For example, consider the array

x: **array** $[0 .. 1, 0 .. 2, 0 .. 3]$ **of** real

its tree representation is shown in figure 3.3.

The advantages of this method of implementation are

(1) the various 'rows' do not have to be contiguous
(2) accessing can be done simply by the addition of subscript values to base addresses, no multiplications are required
(3) it is simple to include array bound checks.

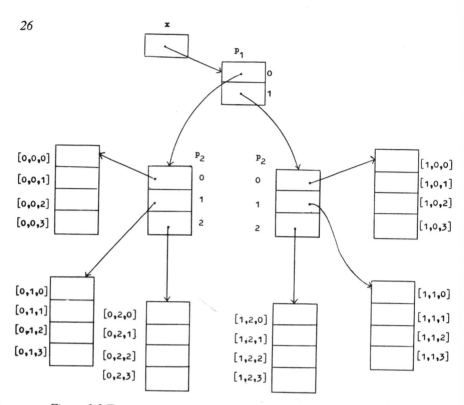

Figure 3.3 Tree representation of x : **array** [0 . . 1,0 . . 2,0 . . 3] **of** *real*

Its disadvantage is, of course, that the descriptors require storage space. The extent of this overhead can be minimised, however, if the subscripts are rearranged so that $p_1 \leqslant p_2 \leqslant \cdots \leqslant p_n$ where p_i is the range of the ith subscript. It is preferable if this optimisation is performed by the compiler.

3.4 SUMMARY

1. An array is a fixed size, finite, set of elements, each element is of the same type and may be individually referenced by the use of subscripts.
2. Arrays are a structured or static representation of functions.
3. Arrays may either be implemented by
(a) the runtime evaluation of the mapping function
(b) the explicit storage of the mapping function as a tree structure.

3.5 BIBLIOGRAPHICAL NOTES

The implementation of arrays is discussed in many books on programming. Well worth reading is the section on arrays in chapter 2 of Knuth's classic book *The Art of Computer Programming*, vol. 1 (Knuth, 1968).

4 *Simple Data Structuring*

4.1 RECORD TYPES

A simple structured type can be formed by the set product† of two or more
unstructured types. The result is known as a **record** type. A familiar example is
the type complex number, which consists of all possible ordered pairs of real
numbers. Thus

      type complex = **record**
                  realpart : real;
                  imagpart : real
                  end

or more briefly

      type complex = **record**
                  realpart, imagpart : real
                  end

define complex numbers to be records with realpart and imagpart components,
and each components is of type real.

We may indicate a complex constant such as $23 + i5$ as

    complex (23,5)

the name of the type being made explicit so as to avoid ambiguity.

Another simple record type is the date, which may be declared

      type date = **record**
                  day : 1 . . 31;
                  mon : month;
                  year : 1900 . . 1999
                  end

where

      type month = (jan, feb, mar,
                    april, may, june,
                    july, aug, sept,
                    oct, nov, dec)

† The set product $U \times V$ of two sets U and V is defined as $\{(u, v)|u \text{ is in } U \text{ and } v \text{ is in } V\}$

If todaysdate is a date variable then we may make the assignment

todaysdate = date (4, sept, 1973)

To allow a simple implementation of record types we cannot exclude any 'unwanted' record values that may occur. Thus type date includes the values

date (31, june, 1944)

The Cobol programmer will recognise in the definition of record types a facility akin to the definition of subordinate data items. Thus the DATA DIVISION entry

```
01  ∅RDER-REC.
    03  ∅RDER-N∅        PIC 9(4).
    03  DESCRIPTI∅N     PIC X(20).
    03  THE-DATE.
        05  THE-YEAR    PIC 99.
        05  THE-M∅NTH   PIC 99.
        05  THE-DAY     PIC 99.
    03  ∅RDER-VAL       PIC 9(6).
```

could be defined with more precision by

```
type orderrec = record
            orderno     : 0 .. 9999;
            description : array [1 .. 20] of char;
            thedate     : record
                        theyear   : 0 .. 99;
                        themonth : 1 .. 12;
                        theday    : 1 .. 31
                        end;
            orderval    : 0 .. 999999
            end
```

Notice that in this example and generally we may use any simple structured type as record components.

The components of a record type variable may be identified for selecting or updating by means of a composite identifier

⟨identifier⟩ · ⟨component-identifier⟩

Thus

z.imagpart := 52.1

assigns 52.1 to the imagpart of complex variables z and

y.realpart := x.imagpart

assigns the imagpart of x to the realpart of y.

For obvious reasons this method of denoting record type components is known as the 'dot-notation'. In some situations it can be tedious to quote the full name of each record component, so we may abbreviate it by use of **with**. The with statement allows the record identifier to be implied, thus

```
with x do
      begin
      realpart :=7.2;
      imagpart := 6.2
      end
```

is equivalent to

```
x.realpart := 7.2;
x.imagpart := 6.2
```

4.2 IMPLEMENTATION OF RECORD TYPES

The standard method of representing a record type value is simply by storing its components in consecutive elements of an array (or region of main store). There is a considerable variation in the amount of padding which may be involved in the juxtaposition. Often each component value is made to occupy an integral number of words or array elements since this provides shortest access times.

For instance a complex variable, x may be represented by

```
array [1 .. 2] of real
```

where $x[1]$ holds the real part and $x[2]$ the imaginary part.

If the values can fit into less storage than one word, then it is possible to pack more than one component into the word. In a tightly packed representation, the bit patterns of the components are directly juxtaposed. In a more loosely packed representation, the components may be fitted within certain subdivisions of a word, which are 'natural' in the sense that special machine instructions are available for selecting or updating particular parts of a word – for example, half word, byte or characters. The disadvantage of packing is, of course, the space and time overhead of having instructions to unpack and repack the data whenever they are accessed.

Whatever implementation is chosen, it is advisable to have an initialisation procedure to preset the value of a record type, when it is declared to a standard value, for example, for complex (0,0).

4.3 USE OF STRUCTURED TYPES

As a simple example of the use of record types, consider the following abstract program to solve a quadratic equation with possibly complex roots.

```
program quadratic-equation;
type complex = record
                realpart, imagpart : real
              end;
```

```
var a,b,c, discriminant, twoa:real,
    x0, x1 : complex;
begin
    .
    .
    .
twoa := 2 * a;
discriminant := b * b − 4 * a * c;
if discriminant < 0 then
                begin
                x0.realpart := x1.realpart := −b/twoa;
                x0.imagpart := x1.imagpart := sqrt(−discriminant)/twoa;
                x1.imagpart := x0.imagpart
                end
else    {discriminant >0, real roots}
                begin
                x0.realpart := (−b + sqrt(discriminant))/twoa;
                x1.realpart := (−b − sqrt(discriminant))/twoa;
                x0.imagpart := x1.imagpart := 0
                end
    .
    .
    .
end
```

The above program is correct for any implementation of complex numbers. The program can be understood in terms of the concepts which arise from the nature of the problem — not the nature of the language or machine to be used. Consider, however, the following Algol 60 program which is the direct equivalent of the one previously given.

```
begin
real a,b,c, discriminant, twoa;
array x0[1 : 2], x1[1 : 2];
comment {x0, x1 : complex, x0[1] = realpart, x0[2] = imagpart, same for x1};
x0[1] := x0[2] := x1[1] := x1[2] := 0;  comment initialise x0, x1;
    .
    .
    .
twoa := 2 * a;
discriminant := b * b − 4 * a * c;
if discriminant <0 then
                begin
                x0[1] := x1[1] := −b/twoa;
                x0[2] := sqrt(−discriminant)/twoa;
                x1[2] := x0[2]
                end
```

else   **begin**
                              comment discriminant $\geqslant 0$, real roots;
                              $x0[1] := (-b + \text{sqrt(discriminant)})/\text{two}a;$
                              $x1[1] := (-b - \text{sqrt(discriminant)})/\text{two}a;$
                              $x0[2] := x1[2] := 0$
                              end

    .
    .
    .

end

   The objection to this program is that our comprehension of it requires
knowledge of

(1) the algorithm for the solution of quadratic equations with possibly
    imaginary roots
(2) the chosen implementation of complex numbers.

   The program is therefore harder to understand, verify and modify, than it
need be. Although this is not much of a problem in the example considered, the
more complex the algorithm and data structures used the greater it becomes.
Languages such as Algol 60 do not allow the definition of new types, so we are
forced to write programs in which the abstract algorithm and language
dependent implementation are intermixed. But this is no excuse for not
designing our algorithm first using abstract types, and then transcribing it into a
programming language using the chosen representation of the abstract types,
carefully keeping as much of the original design as possible. For instance the
readability of the example program would be improved by use of two constant
variables, imagpart = 2, realpart = 1, so that $x0[1]$ could be written $x0[\text{realpart}]$,
etc. The separation in the design process should result in programs in which the
distinction between algorithm and implementation can be seen clearly enough
to be understood separately.

4.4 VARIANT TYPES

In defining structured types it is often useful to be able to form a type from the
union of two types. For instance in a stock control application we may have
different types of update records depending on the nature of the transaction.
The set of values constituting the type update will be the union† of all the
different transaction types.

---

† The union $U\ V$ of two set sets, U, V is defined as

   $\{x \,|\, x \text{ is in } U \text{ or } x \text{ is in } V\}$

Suppose we can distinguish three types of transaction

```
type sales      = record
                    stock no        : integer;
                    dated           : date;
                    quantity        : integer;
                    purchaser code : 0 . . 9999;
                    discount rate   : 0 . . 10
                  end
type purchase = record
                    stock no       : integer;
                    dated          : date;
                    quantity       : integer;
                    customer no : 0 . . 9999
                  end
type misc       = record
                    stock no : integer;
                    dated    : date;
                    quantity : integer;
                    reason   : (loss,gain,return);
                    details  : array [1 . . 20] of char
                  end
```

The type update which comprises values from the union of these three types can be defined by a *variant* record

```
type update = record
                 case trans       : (sales trans, purchase trans, misc trans) of
                 sales trans      : sales;
                 purchase trans : purchase;
                 misc trans       : misc
               end
```

In this example we may take advantage of the fact that several of the components are the same. This may be done by bringing the common components in front of both alternatives.

```
type update = record
                 stock no : integer;
                 dated    : date;
                 quantity : integer;
                 case trans       : (sales trans, purchase trans, misc trans) of
                 sales trans      : (purchaser code: 0 . . 9999;
                                       discount rate: 0 . . 10);
                 purchase trans : (customer no: 0 . . 9999);
                 misc trans       : (reason: (loss,gain,return);
                                       details:array [1 . . 20] of char)
               end
```

The union of several types requires the introduction of an extra component, in the above example

    trans : (sales trans,purchase trans,misc trans)

which is known as the *type discriminant*, its purpose is to identify the variant actually assumed by a variable. This extra 'tag' field is necessary since it must always be possible to select from which of the constituent types it originated. Utmost care must be taken when processing variant records to ensure that the components to be accessed are applicable to the variant actually assumed. If this rule is violated then in the above example we might mistakenly try to update the reason component of a sales-trans variant record. Hence we normally use a **case** statement to process a record variant. In general, a variable declared as

    var x: **record**
        case t : T **of**
        c_1 : T_1;
        c_2 : T_2;
        .
        .
        .
        c_n : T_n
        end

should be processed by a statement of the form

    case $x.t$ **of**
    c_1 : s_1;
    c_2 : s_2;
    .
    .
    .
    c_n : s_n
    end

where s_k is a statement which caters for x assuming the form of variant k. For example

    var currentrec : update

may be safely processed by

    case currentrec.trans **of**
    salestrans   : salesproc;
    purchasetrans : purchaseproc;
    misctrans   : miscproc
    end

4.5 IMPLEMENTATION OF VARIANT TYPES

In representing a value from a variant it is normal explicitly to represent the tag field which indicates from which constituent the value originates. A variant of n alternatives can be represented by an integer in the range 0 to $n - 1$. As with record types there is a choice of the degree of packing used in a representation.

It is possible to omit the tag in the representation of variants and rely on contextual information to know which interpretation is correct. If the programmer is mistaken, this will cause an error that is undetectable by either runtime or compile-time check. Since the effect of such an error will depend on details of bit pattern representation, it will give rise to results unpredictable in terms of the abstractions with which the programmer is working. It would seem that only foolhardiness or exceptional circumstances should lead to the omission of tag fields.

4.6 SUMMARY

1. Records may be constructed from simpler types, for example

```
type date = record
            theyear   : 0 .. 99;
            themonth : 1 .. 12;
            theday    : 1 .. 31
            end
```

The components of record variables are selected by use of the dot notation, for example

```
var today : date
today.theday := 25
```

2. Records are implemented by juxtaposing the components in store, in either a packed or unpacked format.
3. Variant types are records which have components that may assume different structures according a tag field, for example

```
type partmovement = record
                    part no   : integer;
                    quantity : integer;
                    dated     : date;
                    case direction: (in,out) of
                    in   : (supplier: array [1 .. 20] of char);
                    out : (dept     :deptno)
                    end
```

They should be processed in the context of a **case** statement

```
var new transfer : partmovement;
case new transfer.direction of
in   : increase stock process;
out : reduce stock process
end
```

4. Variant types require the explicit implementation of tag fields.

4.7 BIBLIOGRAPHICAL NOTES

Record types were proposed in a paper entitled 'Record Handling' by Hoare (1968). Textbooks on Pascal contain many examples of their use, for example, Jensen and Wirth (1975) or Wirth (1973).

5 On Program Design

5.1 STEPWISE REFINEMENT OF PROGRAMS

Chapter 1 introduced the concept of designing programs by the method of stepwise refinement. In essence, we try to decompose a problem into a simple series of subproblems. Given a problem P, we try to discover a set of smaller problems $P_1, P_2, P_3, \ldots$, such that solving first P_1, then P_2 and so on will be a solution to the original P. This approach is then applied to each of the subproblems $P_1, P_2, P_3, \ldots$, producing a set of sub-subproblems whose solutions taken together are a solution to P_1. We continue this process until the problems are sufficiently small to be capable of solution directly. It is the continual outside-in analysis of the problem which develops the solution to the problem. This analysis and thus the structure of the solution can be usefully represented and guided by a development tree as shown in figure 5.1.

In that each level of the tree ignores the details of the level below it, we may refer to *levels of abstraction* when discussing a solution produced by stepwise refinement.

Each time we develop a level of abstraction which corresponds to a given problem we are, in effect, *refining* the statement of that problem into one with more detail and more indication as to *how* the problem is to be solved. Each step in the refinement, $P_1, P_2, P_3, P_{11}, \ldots$, implies some design decisions which must be carefully considered from two different viewpoints.

(1) Correctness – do correct solutions to P_1, P_2, P_3, always constitute a solution to P?
(2) Feasibility – are solutions to P_1, P_2, P_3 feasible bearing in mind the language or computer to be used?

By the very nature of the design process $P_1, P_2, P_3, \ldots$, will usually be informally specified, thus making the rigorous checking of correctness and feasibility impossible. However, if either is in question the $P_1, P_2, P_3, \ldots$, must be 'firmed up' (if necessary, by tentatively continuing the refinement analysis) until a more rigorous analysis lays the doubts to rest or causes the abandonment of the proposed $P, P_1, P_2, P_3, \ldots$, decomposition.

The discovery of an error during the design process should be considered neither as a random mistake to be fixed and forgotten as soon as possible, nor as a wrongdoing to be subjected to a cover-up by bending the problem specification. Each error should be subjected to the fullest analysis in order to ascertain

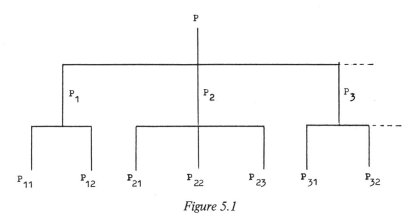

Figure 5.1

(1) the true nature and extent of the error
(2) the misconceptions or unfounded assumptions that led to the error.

Once the true nature of the error is understood, the designer must 'back up' the development tree and redo the refinement process from the first error-free level. Only in this way can the integrity of the final design be safeguarded. Conscious understanding of the causes of the error is an essential element in the experience that differentiates the skilled programmer from the inexpert.

Program design involving as it does the 'unmastered complexity' of an infinite set is very prone to human error. No reasonable safeguard should be omitted by the designer to ensure that he keeps to a minimum the number and scope of the errors he 'designs'.

The temptation to distort program structure in the name of efficiency should be restricted during the design process. It only makes sense to optimise a correct program, whose performance has been measured.

5.2 TWO EXAMPLES

To make clear the idea of stepwise refinement, we shall tackle two programming problems. The first problem is extremely simple; the second, although not difficult, is more representative of real programming problems. In each case it would be beneficial for the reader to solve the problem first.

Example 1: A Sorting Problem

A list of n ($\leqslant 100$) integers is preceded by the value of n. Design a program to read the list and print it, followed by the list sorted in ascending order.

Solution

The problem statement implies three basic operations, readlist, sortlist and printlist. These may be placed in sequence to give an initial solution

```
begin
readlist;
printlist;
sortlist;
printlist;
end
```

Experience of programming tells us the reading and printing of the unsorted list may be done concurrently by printing each integer as it is read. This is not possible in the case of the sorted list, since the printing cannot start until the sorting has been completed. The revised initial solution is therefore

```
begin
read and printlist;
sortlist;
printlist
end
```

The correctness and feasibility of this solution are not in doubt.

Having completed a level of abstraction, we have specified what is to be done; the next question is how? This requires decisions to be made regarding the structure of lists. Clearly arrays are suitable structures since their random access capability makes them suitable for reading, printing and sorting. This choice means the first version can be rewritten in terms of arrays

```
var list : array [1 .. 100] of integer;
     n   : integer;    {number of items in list}
begin
read(n); write(n);  {read and printlist}
i := 1;
while i ≤ n do
       begin
       read(list[i]);
       write(list[i]);
       i := i + 1
       end;
sort list[1] .. list [n] ; {sortlist}
i := 1;
write(n);                   {printlist}
while i ≤ n do
       begin
       write(list[i]);
       i := 1 + 1
       end
```

Clearly sortlist is the next operation due for refinement. When the sort has been completed the largest value in the list will be in position n, the second largest in position $n - 1$, and so on. This suggests an iterative process which, for decreasing m, finds the maximum element in the array elements list[1] .. list[m], and interchanges it with the mth element. We may specify this as

```
m := n;
while m ≥ 2
        do begin
            find maximum of list[1] .. list[m] at maxposn;
            interchange list [maxposn] and list[m];
        end
```

The final stage in the development process is to refine *find maximum* and *interchange*. The simplest method of finding the maximum is to perform a sequential scan of the list

```
max := list[1];                         {find maximum of list[1] .. list[m]
maxposn := 1;                                              at maxposn}
while i ≤ m
        do begin
            if list[i]:
                then begin
                    max := list[i]:
                    maxposn := i
                    end;
            i := i + 1
        end
```

Interchanging can be achieved by

```
temp := list[maxposn]; {interchange list[maxposn] and list[m]}
list[maxposn] := list[m];
list[m] := temp
```

We may put all these fragments together to give

```
var list : array[1 .. 100] of integer;
        n : integer; {the number of items in list}
    m, i, maxposn, max, temp : integer;
begin
read(n); write(n);     {read and printlist}
i := 1;
while i ≤ n do
        begin
        read(list[i]);
        write(list[i]);
        i := i + 1
        end;
m := n;     {sortlist}
while m ≥ 2 do
        begin
        max := list[1];     {find maximum of list[1] ... list[m] at maxposn}
        maxposn := 1;
```

```
while i ≤ m do
    begin
    if list[i] > max
        then begin
                max := list[i] ;
                maxposn := i
                end;
        i := i + 1
        end
    temp := list[maxposn] ;    {interchange list[maxposn] and list[m]}
    list[maxposn] := list[m] ;
    list[m] := temp
    end;
i := 1;    {printlist}
write(n);
while i ≤ n do
    begin
    write (list[i] );
    i := i + 1
    end;
end
```

Example 2: Stock Update and Report Program

A wholesaler keeps details of his stock on a magnetic storage file. Stock levels in the warehouse change as stock is bought, sold, returned, etc. The wholesaler wishes to use information regarding these transactions regularly both to update the stock file and to produce a printed report of stock and transaction information. It has already been decided to produce for this purpose a sequential file containing the transaction information. You are required to design a program which will read the stock file and the transaction file, write the updated stock file and print the report.

(a) *Stock File* The stock file records have the following structure

Field	Type
Stock code number	codenumber
Product name	**array** [0 .. 14] **of** char
Warehouse number	0 .. 1000
VAT rating as a %	real
Unit cost price	0 .. 100000
Unit selling price	0 .. 100000
Stock level	integer

Records are sorted in ascending sequence of stock code number.

(b) *Transaction File* The transaction records have the following structure

Field	Type
Stock code number	codenumber
Date	datetype
Quantity	0 .. 10000
Transaction type	(sale, loss, purchase, return, gain)

The records that have been validated are sorted in ascending sequence of date within stock code number.

(c) *Report Format*

(1) *Heading* Each page of the report carries a heading, where n is the page number 'STOCK REPORT PAGE n'

(2) *Stock Information* Information is printed about each type of stock in order of ascending stock code number and consists of the product name, a list of all transactions on this run for this stock code number in date order, followed by the total change in stock level, value of stock in hand (based on cost price) and profit for this run. A warning message is printed drawing attention to any negative stock level. Transactions for stock codes which do not exist on the stock file are printed with a suitable warning message and rejected.

(3) *Summary Information* The report is terminated by grand totals of stock in hand value and profit on this run.

(d) *Calculation of Profit* The calculations involved in each transaction are described below where q represents quantity, s selling price and c cost price.

Transaction Type	Change in Stock Level	Change in Profit
Sales	$-q$	$(s - c)q$
Loss	$-q$	$-cq$
Purchase	$+q$	0
Return	$+q$	$-(s - c)q$
Gain	$+q$	cq

Solution

The problem specification is typical of many commercial data processing programs. The updating of an old master file to give a new master file is the quintessential data processing job, and also, as in this problem the format and organisation of the files are frequently fixed by the problem specification rather than the programmer. This tends to make systematic program design more difficult, since it pushes low-level issues to the fore thereby obscuring the abstractions central to the production of well-structured programs. When faced with this problem the programmer must be prepared initially to 'back off' from many of the details provided in the specification so as to be able to proceed with stepwise refinement.

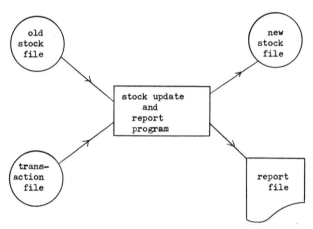

Figure 5.2

The essence of the problem as given is that it maps two input files into two output files (figure 5.2).

To find the underlying structure of the program we initially discard as much detail as possible without destroying the essence of the problem. Clearly we can ignore the details and processing of individual record structures. Another simplification is to assume that the transaction file contains at most one record per stock code. Finally, the ordering of the records is an unnecessary detail at this first level of abstraction. Conceptually at this level the program has, as inputs and outputs, sets of stock codes, and may be reformulated in the following terms.

OS, NS, T and *R* denote the set of stock codes on the old stock file, new stock file, transaction file, and report file respectively. The input to the program is simply the union, $S \cup T$. The desired output can be specified as
for all x in $S \cup T$

(a) x in S, and x in T then put updated (x) in *NS* and put x in R
(b) x in S, but x not in T then put x in *NS* and R
(c) x not in S, but x in T, then put x in R and mark as error.

This can be achieved by a simple and highly abstract program

```
begin
x := get (S ∪ T);
while more in S ∪ T
        do begin
            if x not in T then begin
                            put x in NS;
                            put x in R
                            end
```

```
        else
        if x not in S then put x in R and mark as error
        else begin
                put updated (x) in NS;
                put x in R
                end;
        x := get(S ∪ T)
        end;
  end
```

This 'program' is clearly correct, since it processes all x in $S \cup T$ and deals with all the cases mentioned in the abstract specification.

The solution is made more concrete by the gradual inclusion of all the details given in the problem specification. Thus we are essentially performing a series of refinements in which many of the steps are constrained by the specification. The first 'detail' that should be fed back into the solution is that the program processes two sorted files rather than a single unordered set. The reason for sorting files is to permit the detection of absent stock codes during the course of a single scan through a file. Consequently the program can process the data and produce the output during the course of one simultaneous scan of both input files. Refining the solution to deal with S, T, NS, and R as sorted files gives

```
  begin
  s := get(S);
  t := get(T);
  while not (eof(S) and eof(T))     {while more input}
        do begin
            if eof(T) or s < t then {s is in S, but not in T}
                    begin
                    put s in NS;
                    put s in R;
                    s := get (S)
                    end
            else
            if eof(S) or t < s then {t is in T, but not in S}
                    begin
                    put t in R and mark as error,
                    t := get (T)
                    end
            else begin     {t = s, update s using t}
                put t in R;
                put updated (S) in NS;
                put s in R;
                s := get (S);
                t := get (T)
                end;
            end;
  end
```

The over-all correctness of this program can be established by showing that it is a correct implementation of the previous solution in which unordered sets have been replaced by sorted files. Clearly the **while** loop condition, **not** (*eof* (*S*) *and* eof (*T*)), corresponds to 'more in $S \cup T$'. The single variable x in the abstract program has been replaced by two variables s and t, but it is only one, the smaller of s and t, that is actually processed on each iteration. The eof (*T*) and eof (*S*) conditions quite clearly correspond to cases of 's not in T' and 't not in S', but not so obvious are the $s < t$ and $t < s$ conditions. Their correctness can best be established by considering the state of the input files at the start of an iteration (figure 5.3).

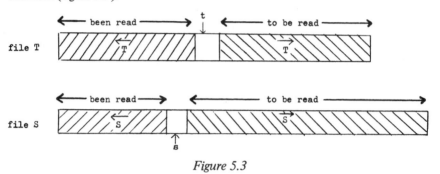

Figure 5.3

Because the files are sorted it can be seen that

all the stock codes in $\overleftarrow{T} < t <$ all the stock codes in $\overrightarrow{T}$

and

all the stock codes in $\overleftarrow{S} < s <$ all the stock codes in $\overrightarrow{S}$

but since the program only processes the minimum of s and t at this point in the program the following conditions are always true

C1: all the codes in $\overleftarrow{T} < s$

and

C2: all the codes in $\overleftarrow{S} < t$

From this it follows that the first **if** condition

$s < t$ implies $s \neq$ all the codes in $\overleftarrow{T}$, t, and $\overrightarrow{T}$, that is, s is not in T

and similarly the other condition

$t < s$ implies t is not in S

A trace through the program will show that C1 and C2 are true on entering the iteration for the first time, and left true after every subsequent iteration for which s and t are defined.

The discussion of correctness has revealed that it is extremely important that both the files are sorted correctly. If there is a stock code out of sequence, on either of the files, then the program will produce an incorrect result, but without giving any explicit sign of having done so. It is therefore imperative that input to the program be performed by procedures that check the ordering of the files and report an error if one occurs. There is no need to terminate execution on the occurrence of a sequence error, they need only be reported in a manner analogous to the reporting of syntax errors by a compiler. The procedures getstock and gettransaction in the next level of refinement perform the task of sequence checking.

Having convinced ourselves of the correctness of the solution so far we must continue the process of making it more concrete. The program can now be developed to handle the full transaction file structure in which there could be more than one transaction with the same code. On reflection there are two possibilities as to how this complexity may be accommodated

(1) the variable *t* could be considered to be a sequence of records with the same stock code. This would limit the changes to the program structure to 'inside' the statements dealing with *t*, that is, 'get (*T*)', 'put *t* in *R*', etc., or
(2) the sequence of transaction records with the same stock code have all to be processed in the same manner, that is, by the same branch of the **if** statement. Which branch may be determined by the first record of the sequence and the sequence may be performed on a one-record-at-a-time basis. Consequently we may include the processing of transaction sequences as simple modifications to the appropriate branches of the **if** statement.

The first alternative looks ahead an entire sequence of transaction records at a time, and therefore requires an indefinite amount of storage to hold it. This alternative is therefore rejected in favour of the second.

At this point in the development, it is necessary to give the file records some minimal structure, since we need to distinguish the codes of records from the information they contain. The old and new stock file records can be considered to be of

```
type stockrec = record
                code : codenumber;
                info : stockinfo
                end
```

and transaction file records to be of

```
type transrec = record
                code : codenumber;
                info : transinfo
                end
```

The report file records are one of three different alternatives, transaction lines, stock totals, or transaction errors, and may be considered as

```
type reportline = record
                code : codenumber;
                case tag : (transaction, total, error) of
                transaction : (info : transinfo);
                total : (info : stockinfo);
                error : (info : transinfo)
                end
```

We need a sequence checking stockfile input procedure which may be specified as

```
function getstock : stockrec;
        var next : stockrec;
        begin
        next := get (S);
        if next.code ≤ lastcode
            then begin
                stockfilerror := stockfilerror + 1;
                write('sequence error, code', nextcode);
                end
            else lastcode := next.code;
        getstock := next;
        end
```

where

```
        lastcode : codenumber
```

and

```
        stockfilerror : integer
```

are global variables. The analogous function gettransaction has a similar structure although it should also check the ordering of the transaction dates.

The resulting program at this level of abstraction is therefore

```
var s : stockrec;     {current old stock record}
    news : stockrec;     {updated new stock record}
    t : transrec;     {current transaction record}
    thiscode : codenumber; {code number of current transaction sequence}
begin
s := get(S);
t := get(T);
while not (eof(S) and eof(T))     {while more input}
    do begin
        if eof(T) or s.code < t.code
            {s.code in S, but not in T, no transactions for this stock}
            then begin
                news := s;
                put(news, NS);
                printtotal (news);
                s := getstock;
                end
```

```
        else
        if eof(S) or t.code < s.code        {t.code in T, but not in S, error}
            then begin
                    printtransaction (t, error);
                    thiscode := t.code;
                    t := get(T);
                    while t.code = thiscode
                            do begin      {sequence of same code records}
                                    printtransaction (t, error);
                                    t := gettransaction;
                                    end;
                    end

        else      {s. code = t.code, update (news) using sequence of transactions}
                begin
                news := s;
                printtransaction (t, ok);
                news := update (news, t);
                thiscode := t.code;
                t := gettransaction;
                while t.code = thiscode
                        do begin      {sequence of samecode records}
                                news := update (news, t);
                                printtransaction (t, ok);
                                t := gettransaction;
                                end;
                printtotal (news);
                put (news, NS);
                s := getstock
                end;
            end;
end;
```

The correctness of this program follows from its direct relationship with the program at the higher level. The important change is the introduction of the loops to process the sequence of transactions with the same stock code number. The structure

```
thiscode := t.code;
t := gettransaction;
while t.code = thiscode
    do begin
            .
            .
            .
        t := gettransaction;
        end;
```

processes such a sequence and correctly leaves *t* containing an unprocessed transaction. It should be noted that the program assumes it is valid to do a get operation when eof is true. If this is not permitted by the filing system then it can be simulated inside the procedures getstock and gettransaction.

There remains a number of loose ends to be tied up by the final stages of the design process. In particular

(1) the details of procedure update, including the processing of the different record types, that is, sales, loss, purchase, return, and gain
(2) the layout of the printlines and the inclusion of page headings and numbers

all need to be specified. However, none of these tasks involves any major refinements or structural changes and they are left to the reader as an exercise.

5.3 SUMMARY

1. The basic idea of stepwise refinement may be described in several different ways

(a) decompose a problem into a sequence of subproblems
(b) refine each statement into several statements with increasing detail
(c) expand what is to be done into a specification of how it is to be done.

2. Make the refinement steps small enough so as to be comprehensible and therefore checkable for correctness.
3. At each step bear in mind the feasibility of the decomposition.
4. After each step, check for errors before proceeding to the next. In the event of an error

(a) find the true nature and cause of the error
(b) back-up to an error-free level and redo the design.

5. In cases where the problem specification includes low-level details of the data representation it may be necessary initially to discard some information to start the refinement process. These details may then be fed back into the solution to control the refinement steps.

5.4 BIBLIOGRAPHICAL NOTES

The books by Wirth (1973 and 1975) contain further examples of the use of stepwise refinement, as does Dijkstra (1972).

Other program design techniques of interest include the method of programming by action clusters (Naur, 1969) and the Jackson method (Jackson, 1975).

Exercises 1

These exercises are mainly simple programming exercises of the kind found in an introduction to programming course. They have been included to provide the reader with an opportunity to try out the method of stepwise refinement using the abstract programming language. The asterisked exercises are referred to later in the book, and it is recommended that they be attempted.

1.1 Although the elimination of **goto**s from existing programs does not usually produce well-designed programs, it is useful to consider how to avoid their use in some of the more frequent awkward cases that can be met when coding. Therefore rewrite the following program control structures without the use of **goto**s.

(a) 'interconnected alternations'

```
label l₁, l₂;
begin
    .
    .
    .
if t₁ then begin
            a;
            if t₂ then goto l₁;
            goto l₂;
            end;

b;
l₁ : c;
d;
    .
    .
    .
l₂ : e;
goto l₁;
end
```

(b) '*n* and a half times round a loop'

> **label** l_1, l_2, l_3;
> **begin**
> .
> .
> .
> l_1 : **if** t_1 **then goto** l_2;
> a;
> **if** t_2 **then goto** l_3;
> b;
> **goto** l_1;
> $l_2 : c$
> l_3 :
> .
> .
> .
> **end**

1.2 Consider the validity of the comment in this program

> **var** a : **array** $[1 .. 10]$ **of** real;
> i : integer;
> **begin**
> $i := 1$;
> **while** $i \leqslant 10$ **do**
>   **begin**
> $a[i] := a[i]/a[1]$;
> $i := i + 1$
>   **end**
> {for $i = 1$ to 10, $a[i]$ has been divided by the original value of $a[1]$}
> **end**

1.3 A darts board consists of the numbered regions 1 to 20; each dart may score one of these numbers and may be doubled or trebled. There are also the inner and outer bull's eye regions which score 25 and 50 respectively. Design a program which, for a given input positive integer value, will output 'yes' or 'no' depending on whether or not it can be scored with a maximum of three darts. If it can, the program should output the individual scores of the minimum number of darts required.

1.4 Design a program that given a positive integer will output in words the value of the integer (the output for 315 should be three hundred and fifteen).

*1.5 A program suite maintains an Outstanding Order Master File which contains all the transactions (that is, the original order and all relevant invoices, credit notes and cancellations) pertaining to each purchase order made by the college that is yet to be completed. The purpose of the program to be designed is to print a report of the contents of this file. The master file consists of a single record for each order, invoice, credit note or cancellation, each record contains

> the value, type, and reference number of the transaction (and in the case of orders a description of the goods is carried)

it also carries information such as

> the nominal code (that is, college department number) to which the transaction applies, the order number of the original order, and the date of the transaction.

The file is sorted in ascending order on order number, nominal code and date. The report program has to print out the contents of the whole file with the outstanding order value shown for every order and for every nominal code within each order. The outstanding value is the sum of the original order value plus the contents of this field in any invoices, cancellations, and credit notes.

1.6 A bank wishes to produce a summary of the transactions made on each account during an accounting period. For each account the bank wants a list showing the balance at the beginning of the period, the number of deposits and withdrawals made, and the final balance.

Each accounts file record contains the account number and the account balance at the beginning of the period. The accounts file is sorted in ascending order of account number.

Each transaction file record contains the account number, the transaction type (deposit or withdrawal) and the transaction amount.

Develop a program for this system when

(a) the transaction file is sorted in ascending order of account number
(b) the transaction file is in random order

1.7 (Jackson, 1975) Design a program to generate and print a multiplication table in the following format

```
 1
 2   4
 3   6   9
 4   8  12  16
 5  10   ·   ·   ·  25
     ·           ·
     ·           ·
     ·           ·
10  20   ·   ·   ·  50   ·   ·   ·  100
```

*1.8 A one-dimensional array of integers

a : **array** $[1 .. m]$ **of** integer

contains an ordered sequence of integers possibly with repetitions. It is required to find the integer which occurs most often in *a*. If the maximum is attained by more than one integer any solution may be given. The resulting value is called the 'mode' of the sequence. For example, in the sequence

(1,1,3,3,3,3,6,7,7)

the value of the mode is 3.

1.9 (Dijkstra, 1972) A character set consists of letters, a space (sp) and a point (pnt). Words consist of one or more but at most twenty letters. An input text consists of one or more words, separated from each other by one or more spaces and terminated by zero or more spaces followed by a point. With the character valued function RNC (Read Next Character) the input text should be read from and including the first letter of the first word up to and including the terminating point. An output text has to be produced, using the primitive PNC(*x*) (Print Next Character) with a character valued parameter, with the following properties

(a) successive words have to be separated by a single space
(b) the last word has to be followed by a single point
(c) when we number the words 0, 1, 2, 3, . . ., in order from left to right, the words with an even ordinal number have to be copied, while the letters of the words with an odd ordinal number have to be printed in reverse order.

For instance, (using '-' to represent a space) the input text

'this--is-a---silly-program-.'

has to be transformed into

'this-si-a-yllis-program.'

Design and implement a program for this problem.

6 *Set Structures*

6.1 INTRODUCTION

So far we have only considered the simple data structuring operations of forming records with or without variants. Although these operations are adequate for many problems they are, by themselves, incapable of expressing clearly the full range of abstractions that can occur in programming.

The purpose of arrays is to express a correspondence between two types. However, we often use them to hold a set of values; for example, we might document the purpose of an array in an operating system simulation program as being 'to hold all the currently available peripherals'. In these cases we are most probably using the array as a means of implementing some other, unmentioned, structured type. Much is to be gained by making all structured types explicit and then considering whether the array is a suitable implementation. In particular we are often disinterested in the order in which the values occur in an array; in this case the **set** is the appropriate abstraction. For this reason our abstract programming language will allow set type variables. A set type is specified by the type declaration

   type T = **set of** T_0

A variable of type T may assume any value which is a set of elements of the base type T_0. Type T corresponds to the powerset† of T_0. Consider the type smallintset

   type smallintset = **set of** 0 . . 3

then the variable x

   x : smallintset

may assume any of the values

   ( ), (0), (1), (2), (3), (0,1), (0,2), (0,3), (1,2), (1,3), (2,3), (0,1,2), (0,1,3), (0,2,3), (1,2,3), (0,1,2,3)

---

† The powerset of some set T_0 is defined as the set of all subsets of T_0, for example, if T_0 = {1,2,3} then powerset (T_0) = {{ }, {1}, {2}, {3}, {1,2}, {1,3}, {2,3}, {1,2,3}}. If the cardinality (number of elements) of set T_0 is n, then the cardinality of powerset (T_0) is 2^n.

In line with the notation for specifying enumeration types we use brackets, ( ), rather than braces { } to enclose set values. This avoids any ambiguity with comments.

Typical set declarations are

type booklist = **set of** book

which might be used in the declaration of variables used to store the books on loan from a library

booksonloan : booklist

or the books recommended for a lecture course

recommendedbooks : booklist

As another example, the allowable peripherals for an operating system could be specified by

type peripheral = (cardreader,cardpunch,lineprinter
                      papertapereader,papertapepunch,
                      console,magnetictape1,magnetictape2)

and thus the current peripheral configuration value would be

configuration : **set of** peripheral

Similarly the in-use and available disc pages for a filing system constitute sets of discpages

available : **set of** discpage
inuse   : **set of** discpage

6.2 SET OPERATIONS

To process set objects we must be able to specify the initial value of all set structured variables and operations for changing them.

The choice of initial value for set variables is conventionally ( ), the empty set, since this provides a simple starting point for any algorithm, and in addition is simple to implement.

The conceptually simplest operation on any types is that of copying or assigning values. After the execution of the assignment

$r := s$

of set variables we may assert that s has remained unchanged and that r has the same value as s. However, as we shall see, the feasibility of implementing assignment efficiently depends largely on the chosen method of implementation, and the size of the set involved.

Without the ability to generate or in some way change non-empty set values we can only write a few interesting programs involving sets. Given a variable s of type

type T = **set of** T_0

we would like to be able to change the value of s by inserting or removing elements of the base type T_0. These basic operations are specified by an extension of the dot notation. To insert a T_0 value, t, into the set s we write

s.insert(t)

which updates the value of s so that we may assert that it now contains the value t. (If s already contains t then the operation has no effect.)

Similarly the operation

s.remove(t)

updates the value of s so that we may assert that it does *not* now contain the element t. (If s does not initially contain t then the operation has no effect.)

The dot notation is used to specify these operations because like the component field selectors of record types they permit a change in the value of a structured variable.

It is also necessary to be able to test set membership — is t in s? For this a suitable notation is

s.has(t)

which returns true if t is a member of s and false otherwise (it always leaves s unchanged).

A final property of sets that is sometimes useful is its cardinality or number of elements. Thus

s.size

returns an integer value corresponding to the cardinality of s.

These basic set operations can be used to construct the more usual set operations of union, intersection and difference.

```
procedure union (a,b : set of 1 .. n; var c : set of 1 .. n);
var i : integer;
begin
i := 1;
while i ≤ n do begin
            if a.has(i) or b.has(i)
              then c.insert(i);
            i := i + 1
            end;
end;
procedure intersection (a,b : set of 1 .. n; var c : set of 1 .. n);
var i : integer;
begin
i := 1;
```

```
while i ≤ n do begin
            if a.has(i) and b.has(i)
                then c.insert(i);
            i := i + 1
            end;
end;
procedure difference (a,b : set of 1 .. n; var c : set of 1 .. n);
var i : integer;
begin
i := 1;
while i ≤ n do begin
            if a.has(i) and not b.has(i)
                then c.insert(i);
            i := i + 1
            end;
end;
```

These algorithms are presented only as proof that insert, remove and has are a functionally complete set of set operations. In practice it is often possible to obtain more efficient functions by using simple variations of these algorithms that take into account the computational cost of the basic operators, insert, remove and has and in addition that it is more efficient to merge a small set into a large one than vice versa.

6.3 USE OF SET STRUCTURES

Many applications of set types arise from the processing of networks or graphs. As a simple example consider the following problem.

A communication system of an organisation can be considered in terms of a directed graph without loops where people are nodes and communication channels are directed arcs (figure 6.1). A node y is *directly reachable* from x iff there exists an arc from x to y as shown in figure 6.2. For each node of a graph there exists a *reachable* set of nodes which can be reached from that node. For example, in the above graph

    reachable(1) = (1,2,3,4)
    reachable(2) = (2,3)
    reachable (6) = (6)

Our problem is to design a program to compute the reachable set for a given node, given the information about which nodes are *directly reachable* from others.

An informal description of the algorithm for constructing the reachable set for some node x is

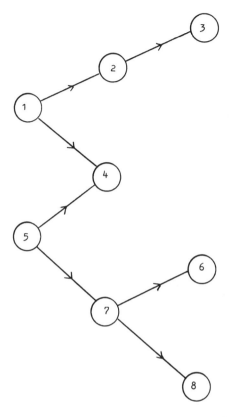

Figure 6.1 Graph of a communication network

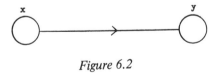

Figure 6.2

(1) put x in the reachable set
(2) repeatedly form the union of the reachable set and all nodes directly
reachable from some node in the reachable set until such time as the total
reachable set is not increased in size.

Without loss of generality we may assume

   type node = 1 .. *n*

where *n* is the number of nodes in the network.

The first stage of the refinement process is to firm up the control structures to be used

```
procedure reachable (x : node; var r : set of node);
    var s : integer;
    begin
    r.insert(x);    {step 1}
    repeat    {step 2}
        s := r.size;
        r := union of r and all the nodes directly reachable from r;
        {on the ith iteration r will contain x and all nodes ≤ i arcs away from x}
    until s = r.size
    end
```

The next refinement to be accomplished is the expansion of

'all the nodes directly reachable from *r*'

as a procedure returning a set of node value

```
procedure directlyreachableset(p : set of node; var r : set of node);
var i,j : integer;
begin
i := 1;
while i ≤ n do    {for all possible nodes 1 .. n}
        begin
        if p.has(i) then begin    {insert all nodes directly reachable from i}
                j := 1;
                while j ≤ n do
                        begin
                        {for all nodes j}
                        if directlyreachable(i,j)
                        then r.insert(j);
                        j := j + 1
                        end;
                end;
        i := i + 1;
        end
    end
```

At this point it is left only to specify the implementation of the boolean function directlyreachable (i,j). This is most easily accomplished for small graphs by the direct array representation of the adjacency matrix of the graph. The adjacency matrix is a mapping

a : **array** [node,node] **of** boolean

such that $a[i,j]$ = true iff node j is directly reachable from node i. The adjacency matrix for the graph used in the example is

node	1	2	3	4	5	6	7	8
1	0	1	0	1	0	0	0	0
2	0	0	1	0	0	0	0	0
3	0	0	0	0	0	0	0	0
4	0	0	0	0	0	0	0	0
5	0	0	0	1	0	0	1	0
6	0	0	0	0	0	0	0	0
7	0	0	0	0	0	1	0	1
8	0	0	0	0	0	0	0	0

Clearly then the final refinement is to specify that the function call

directlyreachable (i,j)

accesses the adjacency matrix element

$a[i,j]$

There is a number of factors which need to be taken into account if this algorithm is to be used on any but small graphs. Not least among the problems is that the adjacency matrix has n^2 elements of which only a few will normally be non-zero.

6.4 IMPLEMENTATION OF SET STRUCTURES

In this section we shall discuss a number of different simple-minded implementations which are often quite adequate for the set types met in practice.

(i) Array Representation of Sets
The simplest representation is to use an array of integers, in which the relevant integers are stored in arbitrary order, with the size of the set being represented stored in an integer. The length of the array, c, constitutes an upper bound on the cardinality of any set value that may be represented. Figure 6.3 illustrates this method of implementation.

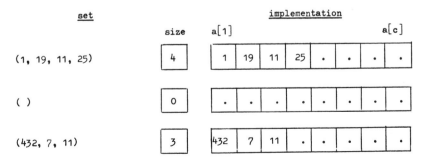

Figure 6.3 The array representation of sets

The implementation of the operations insert, remove and has on

type integerset = **set of** integer;

where the cardinality of the set has some value c as an upper bound is quite simple

```
var a : array [1 .. c] of integer;
size : integer;  {range 0 .. c}
procedure insert(i : integer);
    var j : integer;
    found : boolean;
    begin
    j := 1;
    found := false;
    while j ≤ size and not found do
            begin
            found := a[j] = i;
            j := j + 1
            end
    if not found then    {i is not in a[1] .. a[size]}
        if size < c then begin
                        {make insertion}
                        size := size + 1;
                        a[size] := i;
                        end
                else    {set is full, size = c}
                        error('set a full')
    end;
procedure remove (i : integer);
    var j : integer;
    found : boolean;
    begin
    if size > 0 then begin
                j := 1;
                found := false;
                while j ≤ size and not found
                        do begin
                            if a[j] = i then begin
                                            {do removal}
                                            a[j] := a[size] ;
                                            size := size − 1;
                                            found := true
                                            end
                            else j := j + 1
                            end
                end
    end;
```

```
function has (i : integer) : boolean;
    var j : integer;
        found : boolean;
    begin
    j := 1;
    found := false;
    while j ≤ size and not found do
                    begin
                    found := a[j] = i;
                    j := j + 1
                    end;
    has := found;
    end;
```

The initialisation of the representation to the empty set is accomplished by

size := 0

The correctness of the implementation can only be guaranteed if the global variables array *a* and size are only updated through use of the procedures insert, remove and has. The variable size may be accessed but not changed in order to evaluate the cardinality of the set. The procedure call error ('set *a* full') is assumed to cause an error message to be printed and then cause the termination of program execution by *a* calling a standard operating system function.

The characteristics of this representation are that

(1) it is simple to program and understand
(2) it is efficient in time and space for set values with a sufficiently small upper bound on their cardinality; conversely it is inefficient if this restriction does not apply
(3) the cardinality of the base set is unimportant.

(ii) Bitstring Representation

When the cardinality of the base set is small there is a particularly efficient representation using the hardware bit-by-bit logical functions on computer words.

Consider the representation of the following type on a computer with a sixteen-bit word length.

type smallintegerset = set of 0 .. 15

The state of each of the 16 bits of a word can be used to indicate the absence or presence of each integer in a small integerset value. The value $(0, 5, 9, 11, 13)$ is shown in figure 6.4.

bit number:	0	1	2	3	4	5	6	7	8	9	10	11	12	13	14	15
state	1	0	0	0	0	1	0	0	0	1	0	1	0	1	0	0

Figure 6.4 The set $(0, 5, 9, 11, 13)$

More formally the small integer set value a is represented by the machine word w, wordlength l, if

a.size $\leqslant l$
a.has$(i) \equiv (i$th bit of $w = 1)$

Because most computers provide instructions to do bit-by-bit **and** (&) and **or** ($\oplus$) operations on machine words it is customary to consider the basic updating set operations to be

intersection	w.intersection(v)
union	w.union(v)
difference	w.difference(v)

together with the functional operations

w.has(i)
w.size

$(w, v$ are small integersets, i is an integer) when using the bitstring representation. The implementation of these operations is quite simple, each set is represented by

w : machine word

where conceptually

type machineword = **array** $1 \ldots l$ **of** boolean

The updating operations can be implemented as

```
procedure intersection(v : small integerset);
    begin
    w & v    {bit-by-bit logical and instruction}
    end;
procedure union(v : small integerset);
    begin
    w⊕v      {bit-by-bit logical or instruction}
    end;
procedure difference(v : small integerset);
    begin
    w & (one's complement of v)
    end;
```

Of course, the final choice of implementation will depend on the actual logical bit-by-bit instruction provided by the hardware.

Set membership can be tested by

```
function has(i : 1 .. l) : boolean;
    var x : machineword;
    begin
    x := w;
```

has := **if**(x & (bit code (i)) $\neq$ 0 **then** true
                                        else false
   end;

Bitcode (i) is a machine word value with a value of all zeros except for the bit number i. Bitcode (i) can be implemented by loading a single 1 into bit zero and shifting it right i places. On machines where shifting is slow, a table look up can be used instead.

The size of the set value is the number of one-bits in the machine word. On some machines there is a single instruction for doing this. Where such an instruction is not available the number of one-bits may be computed by shifting left $l - 1$ times and before each shift incrementing a count if the value represents a negative integer value (bit zero indicates the sign on the two's complement, one's complement, and the sign bit representation of integers). A more efficient algorithm is possible, based on the relationship that if x initially contains more than one one-bit then

$$x \ \& \ (x - 1)$$

removes the rightmost one-bit. Care must be taken on some computers since $x - 1$ will cause arithmetic overflow if x is initially negative. The version given here is for a machine with two's complement arithmetic

```
function size (w : machineword) : integer; {range 0 .. l}
    constant mask = 01^(l-1);    {0 followed by (l - 1) one-bits,
                                        masks out sign bit}
    var c : integer;   {range 0 .. l}
        x : machineword;
    begin
    x := w & mask;    {prevent arithmetic overflow}
    if x = w then c := 0   {sign bit was not set}
           else c := 1;   {sign bit was set}
    while x ≠ 0 do begin
               x := x &(x - 1);   {remove rightmost bit}
               c := c + 1
               end;
    size := c
    end;
```

The initial value of the set can be achieved by the assignment

$$w := 0$$

The characteristics of the bitstring implementation are

(1) it is very efficient in terms of storage and time (in effect the hardware is used to perform set operations in parallel)

(2) this method can be easily extended for base types with a size greater than the word length, but if the number of words required is significantly greater than one the attraction of the method disappears.

(iii) Linear Linked Lists

In applications with a large base-set, the size of the sets assumed by a set variable may vary widely during the lifetime of the variable. This will cause unacceptable overheads with the implementations so far discussed. The problem is that each set is allocated a fixed contiguous area of store which is neither easily extended as the set cardinality increases nor shed as the set cardinality contracts.

These problems are usually overcome by the use of linked methods of storage allocation. The available store is split into records called *nodes*, some of which will be linked together to store the elements of some set, and others will be free. The free nodes are also linked together as a free list. Whenever a programmer's set requires extension, a node is acquired from the free list; and whenever an element is removed from the set a node can be returned to the free list.

The simplest form of linked list is the *linear linked list*. Each element of a set is stored in a node; a field of the node — the link field — is used to hold a pointer to (the address of) the next node of the set. The empty set is represented by a value nil which could not possibly be an address (for example, minus one or zero) and the link field of the last node contains this value. A pointer to the first node of the set is stored in a fixed location.

A linear linked list for the integerset $a = (0, 9, 31, 2731)$ is shown in figure 6.5.

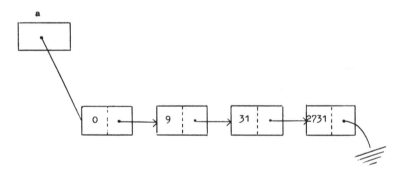

Figure 6.5 The integer set variable a = $(0, 9, 31, 2731)$

One of the more important properties of linked list storage methods is that they allow the dynamic sharing of an area of storage by several variables. We shall discuss linked list storage in depth in a subsequent chapter on advanced data structures.

6.5 SUMMARY

1. Arrays that are documented as 'holding a set of values' are more correctly defined as set structured types.

2. For small sets of any base type, arrays provide an efficient implementation.

3. For sets of a small base type the bitstring method is very efficient.

4. For highly variable sets of any base type a linked storage structure is required.

6.6 BIBLIOGRAPHICAL NOTES

This chapter is based on the treatment of powersets in 'Notes on Data Structuring' (Hoare, 1972b). Some languages substitute the machine level concept 'bits' for set types, for example, Algol 68 (Wijngaarden, 1969).

7 The Class Construct

7.1 USING AND IMPLEMENTING DATA STRUCTURES

The process of stepwise refinement produces programs as a series of levels of abstraction, and at each level the designer is encouraged to ignore the details of the lower levels. Prior to this chapter we have concentrated on the refinement of control structures. But when designing programs, especially large ones, it is also necessary to refine the structure of the data hand in hand with control. Proceeding down the development tree, the designer first postulates and uses a structured type, then at a later or lower level it becomes necessary to specify how it is implemented. Usually the implementation can be arranged in a number of different ways, each with its own strengths and weaknesses. But as far as the higher level is concerned the details of the chosen implementation are irrelevant. If the distinction between the two levels of using and implementing a structured type is blurred then the program structure and transparency must necessarily suffer. It is therefore sensible textually to separate the implementation of a structured type from its use in a program.

The conscious and textual separation of use and implementation makes the understandability, correctness and modifiability of the higher-level abstract program independent of the particular implementation chosen. Similarly the correctness of the implementation can be checked without consideration of the abstract program. The interface between the two remains only the limited concerns of

(1) efficiency – the efficiency of the program will be a function of the implementation
(2) completeness – the implementation must be able to represent all the values evoked by the abstract program. Attempts to represent out of range values must be reported as errors.

As a simple example of how stepwise refinement can lead to the separation of the use of a structured type from its implementation, consider the well known 'Sieve of Eratosthenes' method for generating the set of primes less than some upperbound c. (The importance of the method is that it avoids multiplications and divisions.)

Informally the algorithm can be specified as

step 1: A 'sieve' set is constructed containing all the integers $2 \ldots c$

step 2: Repeatedly

    (a) remove the smallest element from the sieve and add to the set of primes

    (b) remove all multiples of that number from the sieve. The iteration terminates when the sieve is empty.

This first level of abstraction can be refined directly into a program which uses two set structured objects, the working set sieve and the result set primes which is left containing all the primes less than c.

```
const c = ?;   (primes ≤ c)
var j, n, next : integer;   {range 1 . . c}
      sieve, primes : integerset;   {sets of integers 1 . . c}
begin
sieve.init;   {initialise sieve and primes}
primes.init;
j := 2;
while j ≤ c do begin
                sieve.insert(j);
                j := j + 1
                end;
{sieve filled with integers 2 . . c}
while sieve.size ≠ 0 do
                begin
                next := sieve.min;
                primes.insert(next);
                n := next;
                while n ≤ c do
                                begin
                                {remove multiples }
                                sieve.remove(n);
                                n := n + next
                                end;
                end;
end;
```

The next stage in the design process is to find a suitable implementation for the type integerset. The operations to be implemented are

    insert
    min
    remove

of which remove is the most critical because it is used much more frequently than min or insert. For small values of c, the standard array implementation suffices, for larger values of c ($> 10^3$) a different implementation becomes desirable. Now, for the array implementation, the efficiency of the min operation can be improved dramatically if the array elements are kept in ascending order. Unfortunately this can only be done at the expense of making the remove operation 'shuffle down' all the elements after the one removed. This particular variation should not be adopted therefore because remove is more critical than min.

In the next section we shall give the implementation using a notation which allows it to be kept textually separate from the main part of Eratosthenes program.

7.2 CLASSES

The **class** is a construct in some programming languages that allows for the textual separation of the implementation of a structured type from its use. A class for a structured type specifies how all the variables of that type, together with their associated operations, are to be implemented. The syntactic and semantic details of the construct have still to be finalised in the light of practical experience. The notation used here is similar to that used in the experimental language Concurrent Pascal.

We proceed with the refinement of the Sieve of Eratosthenes program to illustrate both the motive and use of the class concept. Both the integer set variables will require separate array and integer size variables together with procedure implementing the operations insert, min and remove

```
var a : array[1 .. c] of integer;
    size : integer;
procedure insert(i : integer)
    begin
        .
        .
        .
    end;
function min : integer;
    begin
        .
        .
        .
    end;
procedure remove(i : integer);
    begin
        .
        .
        .
    end;
```

So that the variables a and size can be accessed by the three procedures they have to be global to the procedures. Furthermore it is clear that to avoid error only these procedures should be used to update the variables a and size.† In traditional languages this protection cannot be enforced by a compiler because any statement that can call one of the procedures can also legally update the variables. The class, however, has scope rules which allow this protection to be provided by a compiler with no runtime overhead. Essentially nothing can be accessed inside a class unless it has the word **entry** immediately preceding it. Thus the implementation of the type integerset can be described by

```
type integerset =                                              (i)
class    {set of integer, cardinality ⩽ c}                    (ii)
    var a : array [1 .. c] of integer;                        (iii)
        entry size : integer;                                 (iv)

    procedure entry insert (i : integer);                     (v)
    var j : integer;
        found : boolean;
    begin
    j := 1;
    found := false;
    while j ⩽ size and not found do
        begin
        found := a[j] = i;
        j := j + 1;
        end;
    if not found then    {i is not in a [1] .. a[size]}
        if size < c then
            begin    {make insertion}
            size := size + 1;
            a[size] := i;
            end
        else    {size = c, set full} error ('set full');
    end;

    function entry min : integer,                             (vi)
        var i, minimum : integer;
        begin
        if size = 0 then error ('minimum of empty sets undefined')
        else begin
            minimum := a[1];
            i := 2;
            while i ⩽ size do
                begin
                if a[i] ⩽ minimum then minimum := a[i];
```

---

† For example, increasing the value of size without inserting a new element in a will lead to unpredictable results.

```
            i := i + 1;
          end;
        min := minimum;
        end;
    end;

  procedure entry remove (i : integer);                           (vii)
      var j : integer;
          found : boolean;
      begin
      if size > 0 then
        begin
        j := 1;
        found := false;
        while j ≤ size and not found do
          if a[j] = i then
            begin     {do removal}
            a[j] := a[size] ;
            size := size − 1;
            found := true;
            end
          else j := j + 1
      end
    end;

  begin     {initialisation}                                       (viii)
  size := 0
  end;     {of class integerset}
```

Line (i): specifies the type being implemented by this class. *Line (ii)*: **class** introduces the class body. *Line (iii)*: **var** introduces the permanent variables of the class, each variable of type integerset has its own set of permanent variables. The permanent variables are global to all the procedures in the class and never go out of existence. *Line (iv)*: permanent variables are inaccessible outside the class unless they are **entry** variables in which case they can be accessed but not changed outside the class. *Lines (v), (vii)*: an **entry** procedure can be called outside the class. *Line (vi)*: an **entry** function can be called outside the class. *Line (viii)*: the initial statement is executed by an explicit initialise statement (init) after declaration of an integerset variable.

The final version of the program for the Sieve of Eratosthenes would therefore consist of the program given earlier together with the above class for the type integerset. Taken together the class and the program provide a compiler with enough information to produce code.

The scope rules of the class construct allow the programmer to regard a structured type as a black box with respect to its implementation. The **entry** variables, procedures, and functions give full control to the implementor in specifying the properties of the structure that are to be transparent to the user.

In addition to the conceptual clarity of textually separating the use of a structured type from its implementation, the compiler can trap all illegal accesses to the implementation details as violations of the scope rules. Consequently a program can be built as a hierarchy of classes. As each new and untested class is added to the program the scope rules ensure that it cannot interfere with the correct functioning of the older and correct classes. Consequently program testing is considerably simplified.

Although classes are not a feature of the commonly available programming languages, they are important as a conceptual device in program design and description. Therefore all the data structures introduced in the subsequent chapters are described in terms of classes.

7.3 IMPLEMENTATION OF CLASSES†

The practical usefulness of classes is enhanced by a scheme for implementing them in the standard languages. As an example we consider their implementation in Pascal.

The black box effect of a class is implemented by declaring each class as a procedure. Objects local to the class are made local to the procedure; the holes in the scope 'wall' together with the storage for each set of permanent variables are effected by passing a single record structured variable to the procedure implementing the class. This parameter also contains fields to determine which class operation is to be performed. In more detail the general rules are as follows.

(1) A **class** for abstract structured type t becomes a **procedure** $t$class (this : t). for example

> **type** integerset
> = **class**
> > .
> > . } class body
> > .
> **end**

becomes

> **procedure** intsetclass (this : integerset);
> > .
> > . } class body
> > .
> **end**

(2) The procedures and functions of the class become the local procedure and functions of the procedure $t$class, for example

† This section may be omitted on first reading.

```
type integerset =
class
        •
        •
        •
    procedure entry insert
        •
        •
        •
    end
    •
    •
    •

end
```

becomes

```
procedure intsetclass (this : integerset);
        •
        •
        •
    procedure insertproc (i : integer);
        •
        •
        •
    end
    •
    •
    •
end
```

(3) The abstract structured type, t, is redefined as a record type which contains fields for (a) the permanent variables of the type, (b) specifying which of the entry operations is to be performed on an invocation of the procedure $t$class, and (c) the necessary parameters for each of the class entry operations; for example

```
type integerset = record
                size : integer;
                a    : array [1 .. c] of integer;
                operation : (init, insert, remove, has);    {class operations}
                arg : integer;    {input for insert, remove, has}
                result : boolean;    {result of has}
                end
```

(4) Each variable of the abstract type t becomes a variable of the record type t, thereby providing a different set of permanent variables for each abstract variable. A class operation on a particular abstract variable is performed by

setting up the fields of the appropriate record type variable and then calling the procedure *t*class; for example

var *x* : integerset;
    i : integer;
  .
  .
  .
x.insert(*i*);
  .
  .
  .

becomes

var *x* : integerset;
    i : integer;
  .
  .
  .
with *x* **do**
    begin
    operation := insert;
    arg   := *i*;
    intsetclass(*x*)
    end
  .
  .
  .

(5) All references, inside the class, to the permanent variables must be prefixed by the name of the formal parameter of *t*class, so that at runtime the correct set is accessed on each call of a class operation; for example

class
var size : integer
    a   : **array** $[1 .. c]$ **of** integer;
  .
  .
  .
if $a[j] = i$ **then**
    .
    .
    .
  .
  .
  .
end

becomes

procedure intsetclass(this : insetclass);

.

.

.

if this .$a[j]$ = i **then**

.

.

.

end

(6) The body of the procedure *t*class must test the operation field of its parameter so as to determine which class operation is to be performed.

procedure intsetclass(this : integerset);

.

.

.

procedure insertproc(i : integer);

.

.

.

procedure removeproc(i : integer);

.

.

.

function hasproc(i : integer);

.

.

.

procedure initproc;

.

.

.

begin   {body of intsetclass}
with this **do**
　　　　begin
　　　　case operation **of**
　　　　insert   : insertproc(arg);
　　　　remove : removeproc(arg);
　　　　has   : result := hasproc(arg);
　　　　init   : initproc
　　　　end
　　　　end;
　　end;

No handcoded implementation of a programming construct can be as secure as a compiler implementation, nevertheless a handcoded implementation still provides the conceptual advantages of abstract design using classes. The method described above can be applied to other languages as well as Pascal; in particular it is well suited to assembler languages.

We conclude this section with a handcoded Pascal version of the Sieve of Eratosthenes program.

```
program eratosthenes(input,output);
{
computes primes in range 1 .. c
using the sieve of eratosthenes
}
const c = ?
type set op type = (init,inset,remove,print,min);
        integerset = record
                   size      : integer;
                   a         : array [1 .. c] of integer;
                   operation : set p type;
                   arg       : integer;
                   result    : boolean
                   end;
var n, j, next    : integer;   {range 1 .. c}
    sieve, primes : integerset;
{
class integerset
operations    : .init                   //initialise
              .insert  (i : integer) //insert i in set
              .remove (i : integer) //remove i from set
              .min                     //return minimum of set
              .print                   //printset
max cardinality = c
}
procedure intsetclass (var this : integerset);
{
i is in set iff there is a j such that
a[j] = i and 1 ⩽ j ⩽ size
and 0 ⩽ size ⩽ c
}
    procedure initialproc;
        begin
        this.size := 0;
        end;
    procedure insertproc (i : integer);
        var j : integer;
            found : boolean;
```

```
begin
with this do
    begin
    j := 1;
    found := false;
    while (j ≤ size) and not found do
        begin
        found := a[j] = i;
        j := j + 1
        end
    if not found then     {i is not in a[i] .. a[size] and
                                            j = size + 1}
        if size < c then begin
                        {make insertion}
                        size := size + 1;
                        a[size] := i
                        end
        else writeln ('set full error');
    end
end;
procedure removeproc (i : integer);
    var j : integer;
        found : boolean;
    begin
    with this do
        begin
        if size ≥ 0 then begin
                        j := 1; found := false;
                        while (j ≤ size) and not found do
                            if a[j] = i then
                                    begin
                                    {do removal}
                                    a[j] := a[size];
                                    found := true;
                                    size := size - 1
                                    end
                            else j := j + 1;
                        end;
        end
    end;
procedure printproc;
    var i : integer;
    begin
    with this do
        begin
        writeln ('set(**');
```

```
                i := 1;
                while i ⩽ size do begin
                                writeln('      **', i : 5, '=', a[i]);
                                i := i + 1;
                                end;
                writeln ('     **) end');
                end;
        end
function minproc : integer;
        var i, minimum : integer;
        begin
        with this do
                begin
                if size = 0 then
                        begin
                        writeln ('error-minimum of empty sets undefined'):
                        end
                else begin
                        minimum := a[1] ;
                        i := 2;
                        while i ⩽ size do
                                begin
                                if a[1] ⩽ minimum then minimum := a[1] ;
                                i := i + 1
                                end;
                        minproc := minimum
                        end;
                end;
        end;
{body of procedure intsetclass}
begin

with this do begin
        case operation of
                init      : initialproc;
                insert    : insertproc(arg);
                remove    : removeproc(arg);
                print     : printproc;
                min       : result := minproc;
        end;
end;    {end of class integerset}

begin
        with sieve do begin
                        operation := init;
                        intsetclass (sieve)
                        end;
```

```
          with primes do begin
                    operation := init;
                    intsetclass (primes)
                    end;
          j := 2;
          while j ≤ c do
              begin
              with sieve do
                  begin
                  operation := insert;
                  arg := j;
                  intsetclass (sieve);
                  end;
                j := j + 1;
              end;
          {set sieve = set(2 .. c)}
          while sieve.size < > 0 do
                  begin
                  with sieve do begin
                            operation := min;
                            intsetclass (sieve);
                            next := result
                            end;
                  with primes do begin
                            operation := insert;
                            arg := next;
                            intsetclass (primes);
                            end;
                  n := next;
                  while n ≤ c do
                      begin
                      with sieve do
                          begin
                          operation := remove;
                          arg := n;
                          intsetclass (sieve);
                          end;
                      n := n + next
                      end;
              end;
          writeln ('primes in range 1 .. ', c : 4, '...');
          with primes do begin
                    operation := print;
                    intsetclass(primes)
                    end;
          writeln ('end of program');
end.
```

7.4 SUMMARY

1. Classes provide a means of defining the implementation of abstract data structures.

2. Their use allows the textual separation of the correctness of a data structure implementation, from the correctness of the program using it.

3. As a language feature, classes allow a program to be developed and tested as a hierarchy of components. New (and untested) components cannot cause old (and tested) components to fail, since illegal accesses can be trapped by the compiler.

4. Classes can be conveniently handcoded into any language that allows procedures.

7.5 BIBLIOGRAPHICAL NOTES

The class concept derives from SIMULA 67 (Dahl *et al.*, 1970). This chapter is based on Hoare (1972a) but using a notation similar to that of Concurrent Pascal (Brinch Hansen, 1975a, 1975b). The method of implementing classes in ordinary Pascal was suggested by the method used in the kernel of the SOLO operating system (Brinch Hansen, 1976).

8 *Dynamic Data Structures*

8.1 INTRODUCTION

Much of our experience in both programming and the real world concerns the manipulation of the 'small rather than the large'. For this we are to be thankful, for once we depart the realm of the small, many trivial operations take on a frightening complexity requiring painstaking organisation. The lifting of an object weighing 1 kg is trivial, 50 kg is difficult but possible, 2500 kg is, for the average human, impossible. A 'mere' quantitative change causes a qualitative change in the nature of the problem. We must expect therefore that once we include the 'large' in a problem we are most likely introducing with it a number of difficulties. This certainly applies to data structures which are in some sense 'large'.

Until now we have only dealt with the small and relatively simple structures which are capable of efficient representation and manipulation on modern computers. Their smallness provides an upper bound on their storage requirements and hence on the storage and time requirements of any algorithm that processes them. Once we allow types with very large or infinite cardinality we are dealing with *advanced data structures*.

The distinction between 'small' finite types and 'large' unbounded or infinite types is of fundamental importance in programming just as the distinction between finite and infinite sets is in computational theory. The decision therefore to define and manipulate types which are unbounded is not to be taken lightly. For instance our programs normally only deal with integers within a certain finite range. If this range is larger than that defined by the machine's architecture, or worse still, is actually unbounded, then a qualitatively more complex and sophisticated representation becomes necessary.

The computational requirements of an infinite or large cardinality type cause problems in two related ways.

(1) Static: both large and small values must be capable of efficient representation and processing.
(2) Dynamic: the variation; at runtime, between small and large values must be efficient.

In many cases, variables of an unbounded type have only a limited dynamic nature. A particular instance of such variables is sequential *files*. Files are essentially only updated by appending information at one end. They have lifetimes in excess of the program that creates or processes them and therefore usually reside on backing store rather than main store. Although theoretically it may be argued that the storage medium is unimportant, it does have major practical consequences because any representation will have to take account of the physical characteristics of the device, for example, transfer speed, head movement, possibility of updating, etc. For this reason we shall not consider further in this book the implementation of file structures but concentrate on main store structures.

When structures can be wholly accommodated in main store the most difficult problem is dealing with the dynamic variation in size of values. The operation central to such *dynamic data structures* is assignment. Consider the simple cross-assignment

$$x := y$$

which results in the duplication of the value held by y. In contrast to unstructured types, the costs of making such a duplicate may not be negligible. An obvious economy is to allow x and y to share the same instance of the value. In other words the value originally known only by the name y now also has the name x. In main store this may be achieved simply by use of indirect addressing or pointers (figure 8.1).

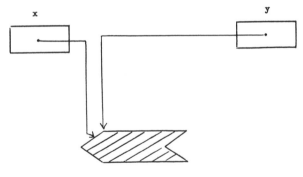

Figure 8.1

Very often assignments share a common variable between their left- and right-hand sides, that is, they are of the form

$$x := f(x, y)$$

In the case of large values it is more efficient to update only the changed individual components of x's existing value rather than to assign a fresh value to the entire structure in a new location.

That is to say, assignment by updating changes x's value (figure 8.2) by changing components rather than by discarding the old structure and acquiring a new one (figure 8.3).

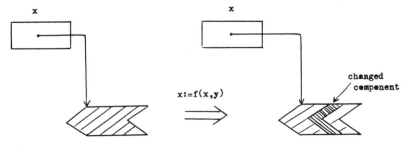

Figure 8.2

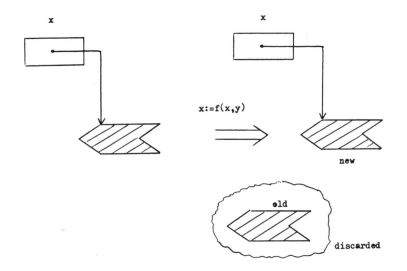

Figure 8.3

In general, the old and new values will have different storage requirements and this will have to be handled by a *storage management* system.

Unfortunately assignment by value sharing and assignment by updating do not co-exist peacefully in the same program. If we have two variables sharing the same instance of a value (figure 8.4) updating either x or y will cause, as a side-effect, a simultaneous change in the value of the other. Such side-effects can be very difficult to detect directly from the program text, thereby giving programs a capricious and unpleasant character. It is inadvisable to combine the two techniques, except perhaps as an optimisation in a program known to be correct.

We shall concentrate on selective updating since it is more generally useful because $x := f(x, y)$ type assignments are more frequent than simple cross-assignments. In fact the dot notation for classes was introduced especially to indicate structure updating.

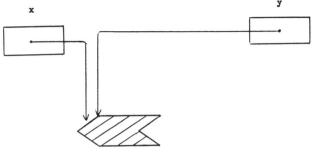

Figure 8.4

8.2 BASIC IMPLEMENTATION TECHNIQUES FOR DYNAMIC DATA STRUCTURES

The main requisite for advanced data structures is the ability to acquire extra store during program execution. We shall follow the notation of Pascal by allowing the generation of dynamic variables by use of a procedure *new*. New introduces a *pointer* value which is the address of the newly allocated variable. A pointer type P is a (finite) set of values pointing to elements of a given type T; P is said to be bound to T. The value *nil* is always an element of P and points to no element at all. Pointer types are bound to a type by use of the symbol '↑'. Thus if we have some type

```
transaction = record
              type    : (sale, purchase, loss, misc);
              quantity: integer;
              value   : sterling;
              code    : stockcode;
              end
```

then we can introduce its associated pointer type by

    type reftransaction = ↑ transaction

and a pointer variable by

    var transptr : reftransaction

or more directly by

    var transptr : ↑ transaction

We denote the pointer value itself by

    transptr

and where transptr points (that is, the variable of type transaction) by

    transptr ↑

To acquire a new variable of type transaction we invoke the call new(transptr) which assigns the address of the new transaction variable to transptr (figure 8.5).

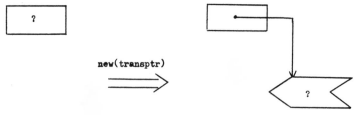

new(transptr)

Figure 8.5

   Although new is a standard Pascal system procedure, it is capable of a simple implementation in any language. The area from which dynamic variables are allocated is known as a *heap* and may be considered to be an array

   heap : **array**[1 .. *n*] **of** machineword

The start of the portion of the heap currently available for allocation to dynamic variables is indicated by the value of the heap top

   var heaptop : 1 .. *n*

Each call on new returns the current value of the heaptop and then increases its value by the number of words required to store the variable pointed to. A call on new when

   heaptop $>$ (*n* − size of dynamic variable)

is an error condition.

   Pointers are essentially an implementation technique for dynamic data structures. They are a powerful concept, but because of the ever present possibility of side-effects due to accidental value sharing they are also potentially dangerous and must be handled with care.

8.3 LINEAR LINKED LISTS

Linear linked lists were informally introduced in chapter 6 on set structures. An unbounded integerset may be represented by a single linked list, or chain of nodes, each node containing a single element. Thus the integerset
$x = (2, 4, \ldots, 10, 15)$ may be represented as shown in figure 8.6.
   The definitions necessary for linear linked lists as the implementation of integersets are

```
type list  = ↑ node;
     node =  record
               value : integer;   {contains element}
               link :↑ node;
             end
```

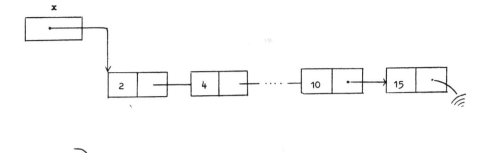

indicates nil

Figure 8.6 Linear linked list for $(2, 4, \ldots, 10, 15)$

Although type list is synonymous with ↑ node we shall reserve the type list for whole lists representing complete structures such as integersets and use ↑ node when we require auxiliary pointers. This distinction is purely for our benefit and we may freely assign ↑ node values to list variables, etc.

Linear linked lists lend themselves to the simple operations required by integersets, as long as the cardinality is fairly small.

Searching a linear linked list, *l*, may be simply accomplished by

```
var l : list;        {head of linked list}                              (i)
    p : ↑ node;      {auxiliary pointer}
found : boolean;
begin
p := 1;                                                                 (ii)
found := false;
  while p ≠ nil and not found
        do if p ↑ .value = i                                            (iii)
              then found := true
              else p := p ↑ .link;                                      (iv)
  if not found then print ('not in l')
               else print ('found at node p ↑');

.
.
.

end
```

Lines (*i*), (*ii*), (*iii*), (*iv*): *p* is an auxiliary pointer used to scan the list; it is initially set to point to the front node on the list; if the value of the currently scanned node is *i* then the search is terminated, otherwise *p* is stepped on one link until the end of the list (*p* = nil) is reached.

The simpler loop

while $p \neq$ nil **and** $p \uparrow$ .value $\neq i$ **do** $p := p \uparrow$ .link

is unacceptable as an alternative because $p \uparrow$ .value is undefined when p = nil.

The updating of a linear linked list, *l*, by the insertion of a new node at its front, can be achieved by the sequence

> new(*p*);
> *p* ↑ .link := *l*,
> *l* := *p*

where, as before, *p* is an auxiliary pointer. Diagrammatically the effect of the execution of these statements is shown in figure 8.7.

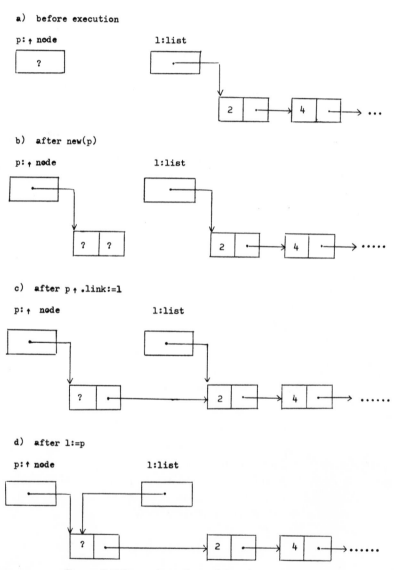

Figure 8.7 Execution of new (*p*); *p* ↑ .link := *l*; *l* := *p*

The single operation

$$l := l \uparrow .link$$

deletes the front node of the linear list. The original value of l must be saved in an auxiliary pointer if the storage occupied by the front node is not to be lost to the program.

8.4 STORAGE MANAGEMENT FOR DYNAMIC DATA STRUCTURES

The heap, through the procedure new, provides a mechanism for dynamic store acquisition. A procedure — dispose — is available in some Pascal implementations for returning store to the heap as it goes out of use. A system 'garbage collector' facility is needed to implement dispose and this tends to be rather expensive. For many applications it is more efficient for the programmer to interpose a store manager or reservoir between his program and the heap. Indeed a reservoir is essential for efficient store utilisation if there are multiple lists of the same type and dispose is not implemented. In this section we deal with a particularly simple store management system which is applicable as long as no attempt is made to return a shared node to the reservoir. If a program uses lists with a variety of node sizes, a separate reservoir is required for each size.

The reservoir is a data structure comprising a *free list* of nodes and the operations initialise, acquire and return. Whenever a program list requires a new node, one is acquired from the free list, and when a node is no longer required it is returned to the free list. The free list is set up as part of the program initialisation sequence and obtains enough store from the heap to meet, at any time, the total storage requirements of all the program lists.

```
type reservoir =
class {nodes with single integer field}
var i      : integer;      {auxiliary integer}
    head : list    ;      {free list}
    t      : ↑ node;      {auxiliary pointer}
function entry acquire : node;
        var t : ↑ node; {auxiliart pointer}
        begin
        if head = nil then error('freelist empty') else t := head;
        head := head ↑ .link;      {have unchained front node}
        t ↑ .link := nil      ;      {disconnect t fully from freelist}
        acquire := t      ;
        end;
```

```
procedure entry return(r :↑ node);
    begin
    if r ≠ nil then begin {a node to return}
                    r ↑ .link := head;
                    head    := r
                    r := nil
                    end
    end;
begin {initialisation sets up freelist with n nodes}
    i := 1;
    head := nil;
    while i ≤ n do begin
                    new(t)          ; {get new node}
                    t ↑ .link := head; {link it in}
                    head    := t   ;
                    i := i + 1
                    end
end {of class reservoir}
```

8.5 LINEAR LINKED LIST IMPLEMENTATION OF INTEGERSETS

We conclude this chapter by returning to our old friend **class** integerset and showing how it may be implemented using linear linked lists. In contrast to all previous implementations we shall model dynamic integersets, that is, the size of set variable will be unbounded and any integer may be used as an element.

The basic updating operations on lists are add a node (with known value) to the front of a list and delete the front node of a list

```
procedure addfront (i : integer; var l : list);
{adds a new node, value i, to front of list l}
var t :↑ node;
begin
t := free.acquire;
t ↑ .link := l     ;
l := t             ;
l ↑ .value := i    ;
end;


procedure deletefront (var l : list);
{deletes front node of list l}
var t :↑ node;
begin
if l ≠ nil then begin
                t := l;
                l := l ↑ .link;
                free.return(t)
                end
end;
```

In addition to these procedures we shall access lists, using auxiliary list pointers of type ↑ node. But modification of list structures will only be performed, by using addfront and addend.

Our implementation of integersets will use selective updating, and as a consequence consideration must be given to the problem of integerset assignment. Let x and y be two integersets

var x, y : integerset

then if the simple assignment

$x := y$

is implemented directly as the assignment of list values

$x := y$ $\{x, y : \text{list}\}$

the result will be a shared structure, and not a fresh copy of the list y (figure 8.8).

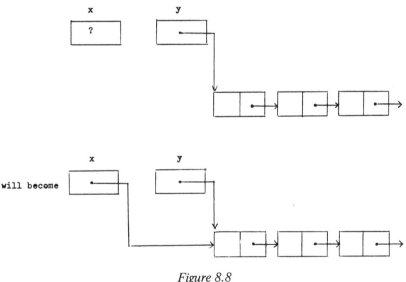

Figure 8.8

A way around this is to consider the definition of integerset assignment in terms of primitive integerset operations and implement it accordingly

var x, y : integerset;

$x := y \Leftrightarrow$ **for** $i := y.\text{min}$ **to** $y.\text{max}$ **do if** $y.\text{has}(i)$ **then** $x.\text{insert}(i)$

where $y.\text{min}$ and $y.\text{max}$ give the minimum and maximum valued elements of y. Generally speaking this is unnecessarily inefficient, especially if the cardinality of y is small compared to the range $y.\text{min} .. y.\text{max}$.

A more efficient solution is to write an integerset assignment procedure which uses the list operation addfront to make a fresh copy.

Although copying lists is a simple concept, a 'make a copy' algorithm might appear difficult to formulate, once it has been realised that the obvious solution

```
var a, b : list;        {make a copy of b in a}
      q : ↑ node;       {auxiliary pointer}
a := nil;
q := b ;
while q ≠ nil
    do begin
        addfront (q ↑ .value, a);
        q := q ↑ .link
        end;
```

in fact makes a reverse copy. However, a recursive solution can be obtained from the following considerations. A list *a* is an exact copy of list *b* if either both the two lists are empty (figure 8.9) or if *a* ↑ .value = *b* ↑ .value **and** the list *b* ↑ .link is an *exact copy* of the list *a* ↑ .link (figure 8.10).

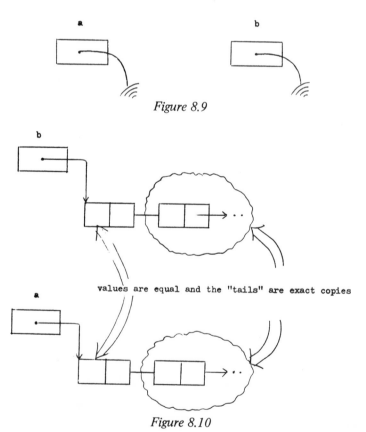

Figure 8.9

values are equal and the "tails" are exact copies

Figure 8.10

Turning this into a constructive procedure we can specify the copy function as

```
function copy(b : list) : list;
        {returns a pointer to a fresh copy of the list b}
        begin
        if b = nil then copy := nil
                else addfront (b ↑ .value, copy(b ↑ .link))        (i)
        end
```

Line (*i*): make a copy of b ↑ .link and then add a new node at its front with value = b ↑ .value.

The function copy is recursive because it is partially defined in terms of itself; this is quite natural for a recursive structure like linear linked lists; a list is defined as a pointer to a node, and nodes themselves are defined in terms of pointers to nodes. When first met, recursion often appears somewhat 'mind-bending' due to the near circular form of the definition. A later chapter will discuss recursion in detail so at this point we shall limit ourselves to the following observations.

(1)　Recursive definitions are not circular — there is always a non-recursive path through the algorithm.

(2)　Recursion is best understood by static or inductive reasoning, for example
　　(a)　does it work for lists with zero nodes?
　　(b)　if it works for list with n nodes will it work for lists with $n + 1$ nodes?
　　If the answer to (a) and (b) is yes then it works for all lists with $n \geqslant 0$ nodes.

(3)　The dynamic behaviour of recursive algorithms is often confusing to follow; however, their implementation is generally simple. Many programming languages allow recursive procedures, for example, Pascal, Algol 60, Algol 68 and PL/I.

For the sake of completeness we give an iterative version of the function copy

```
function copy(b : list) : list;
var a, r : list;
        q : ↑ node;                              {auxiliary pointer}
begin
q := b;
a := nil;
r := nil;
while q ≠ nil do begin {copy reverse (b) into r}              (i)
                addfront (q ↑ .value, r);
                q := q ↑ .link;
                end;
while r ≠ nil do begin {copy reverse (reverse (b))into a}      (ii)
                addfront (r ↑ .value, a)
                deletefront (r);
                end;
copy := a
end
```

Line (*i*): this loop copies *b* into *r* with the nodes in reverse order. *Line* (*ii*): the second loop copies *r* into *a* with the nodes in reverse order. The procedure deletefront releases the nodes of the intermediate list *r*, and sets $r := r \uparrow$ .link.

This function is more cumbersome than the recursive version and is not so simple to understand. For these reasons the recursive version is to be preferred.

Because the assignment of integersets is an operation which has to be explicitly implemented, it has been included as a class procedure. To conform to the notation, the integerset assignment

$$x := y$$

is treated as if it were of the form

$$x.\text{assign}(y)$$

```
type integerset =
class {set of integers, unbounded cardinality}
var entry l : list;                                          (i)
    entry size : integer;
        p : ↑ node;                              {auxiliary ptr}
    function isinlist (i : integer) : boolean
        {scans list for i, if present returns true, uses global pointer p}
        var found : boolean;
        begin
        found := false;
        p      := 1;
        while not found and p ≠ nil
                do if p ↑ .value = i   then found := true
                                       else  p := p ↑ .link;

        isinlist := found;
        end;
    procedure entry assign(y : integerset);
        begin
        size := y.size;                                      (ii)
        l    := copy(y.l)
        end;
    procedure entry insert(i : integer);
        begin
        if not isinlist(i) then begin
                        addfront (i, l);
                        size := size + 1
                        end

        end;
    procedure entry remove(i : integer);                     (iii)
```

```
    begin
    if isinlist(i) then begin {do removal of front node }
                 p ↑ .value := l ↑ .value;
                 deletefront (l);
                 size := size − 1
                 end;
    end;
procedure entry has(i : integer);
    begin
    has := isinlist(i)
    end;
begin
l.init; size := 0;
end {of class integerset}.
```

Lines (*i*), (*ii*): *y*.size and *y*.*l* are the permanent variables, size and *l*, of the parameter integerset *y*. They may be accessed (but not altered) because they are both **entry** variables. *Line* (*iii*): because it is only simple to delete the front node of a list, the removal of an element, *i*, is achieved by overwriting *i* by the front element and then deleting the front node.

Linear linked lists are capable of implementing fully dynamic set structures. The size of the set that can be represented is limited only by the size of the reservoir. They are more efficient storewise than array implementations because their store requirements are proportional to

$$\max\left(\sum_{i=1}^{n}\right)\text{size}_i(t)$$

where *n* is the number of sets and $\text{size}_i(t)$ the size of the *i*th set at time *t*. This value will generally be smaller than the corresponding array implementation requirement

$$\sum_{i=1}^{n}\max(\text{size}_i(t))$$

There are timewise limitations on the efficiency of the method if the average size of each set at each point in time is significantly larger than 70 or 80 elements. At that size it is worth considering the use of linked structures that will support more efficient search methods.

Many of the simplifications in the programming of linear linked lists have been possible because sets are unordered collections of elements. Set structures that exhibit a linear ordering are known as *sequences* and are the subject of the next chapter.

8.6 SUMMARY

1. Advanced data structures result from unbounded types.

2. Dynamic data structures are necessary when variables may hold values of widely differing size, consequently such structures require a store management system.

3. The assignment operation for advanced data structures may be economised by value sharing or by updating; normally updating is the more useful technique. It is unsafe to use both techniques together.

4. Pointers are an implementation technique for dynamic data structures. They must be handled with care because of the ever present possibility of side-effects due to accidental value sharing.

5. Linear linked lists are a suitable implementation for dynamic set structures of average size up to 70 or 80 elements. After that more sophisticated structures become increasingly worth while.

8.7 BIBLIOGRAPHICAL NOTES

The general references for this chapter are the books by Knuth (1968) and Wirth (1975).

Also of interest are the early general linked list processing languages, for example, IPL-V (Newell and Tonge, 1960), LISP (Woodward and Jenkins, 1961) and WISP (Wilkes, 1964).

The concept of advanced data structures is discussed in Hoare (1972b). Value sharing and updating are considered in Hoare (1975); this paper also considers the problems associated with pointer variables.

9 *Sequences*

9.1 INTRODUCTION

At the end of the last chapter it was pointed out that when processing set structures we are not concerned with the order in which elements are stored or accessed. Frequently, however, the ordering is significant; thus character strings are more than sets of characters — the ordering is vital

   'tea', 'eat', and 'ate'

are all distinguishable as strings whereas

   (t, e, a), (e, a, t) and (a, t, e)

are equivalent as sets.
   Unbounded set structures in which the elements or *items* are subject to a linear ordering are known as *sequences*. Typical sequence structures are

   type string = **sequence of** character

and (on backing store) sequential data files

   type datafile = **sequence of** datarecord

The general form of a sequence type definition is

   type T = **sequence of** T_0

where T_0 is the base type. (See figure 9.1.)
   The zero element of a sequence type is the empty sequence which contains no items and is denoted by ( ); sometimes it is also convenient to use λ to denote the empty sequence. For each value v in the base type T_0, there is a sequence whose only element is v and is denoted by (v). Finally, if $v_1, v_2, \ldots, v_n$ are values from T_0 (possibly with repetition), then $(v_1 \, v_2 \ldots v_n)$ denotes the sequence of these values in the stated order. The item v_1 is the *first element* of the sequence which is at the *front* of the sequence; similarly v_n is the *last* element which is at the *end* of the sequence. This notation is dropped in favour of string quotes when manipulating sequences of characters. The set of values in

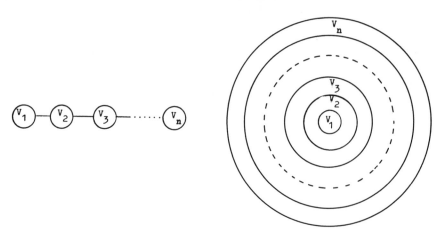

Figure 9.1 Sequences can be represented diagrammatically by a chain or nested hierarchy

a sequence type is exactly the Kleene star[†] (or closure under concatenation) of the base type T_0. For example a variable

 s : **sequence of** ('*a*', '*b*')

may assume any value belonging to the set

 ('*a*', '*b*')*

which, omitting string quotes, is the infinite set (λ, *a, b, aa, ab, ba, bb, aaa, aab,* . . .). It is well known that the Kleene star of a set, $T = (\langle item \rangle)^*$, can be defined by a right linear recursive BNF grammar

 $\langle T \rangle ::= \langle empty \rangle \mid \langle item \rangle \langle T \rangle$

 $\langle empty \rangle ::= \lambda$

By analogy therefore we may regard a sequence definition

 type T = **sequence of** item

as if it were shorthand for a form of recursive schema for type definitions

 rectype T = **record** {sequence of item}
      case tag : (empty, nonempty) **of**
      empty : ( );

[†]The Kleene star of set R, R^*, is defined as

 $R^* = (\lambda) \cup R \cup R^2 \cup R^3 \cdots$

where $R^2 = R.R$, etc. It consists of all finite strings that can be constructed using the elements of R.

```
nonempty : record {type node}
          first : item;
          finalpart : T
          end;
end;
```

The definition depicts a nonempty sequence as a first item followed by a subsequence (figure 9.2) and is therefore most appropriate when the sequence is being processed in a front-to-end direction. Reversing the order of the fields in the nonempty alternative corresponds to the reverse order, that is, end-to-front, processing

```
rectype T = record {sequence of item}
          case tag : (empty, nonempty) of
          empty : ( );
          nonempty : record {type node}
                    initialpart : T;
                    last : item
                    end;
          end
```

(See figure 9.3.)

There does not seem to be a single suitable structure definition that reflects both forwards and backwards processing of sequences. In general we shall assume that both definitions are equally valid, though many implementations only support processing in one direction or the other. An important point is that both definitions are recursive, and hence operations on sequences often have a simple recursive formulation; but it should be borne in mind that the iterative solution is often simpler.

The sequence is fundamentally a generalisation of character strings in which the items can be other than type character. Consequently the basic sequence

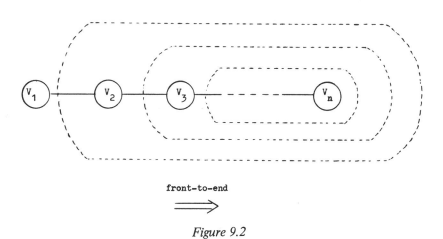

front-to-end
$\Longrightarrow$

Figure 9.2

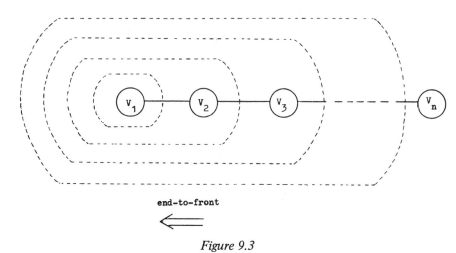

end-to-front

Figure 9.3

operations are the analogues of the basic string processing operations. In particular the primitive sequence updating operations are those of appending or deleting an item at the front or end of a sequence, since these correspond to the left or right concatenation (or deletion) of a character to (or from) a string. The possibility of more complex or random access operations such as the insertion, deletion, or replacement of subsequences at arbitrary points in a sequence will generally depend on the chosen sequence implementation. However, as their name suggests, sequences are always best processed in a sequential rather than a random access fashion.

Before proceeding with a discussion of sequence operations it is appropriate to emphasise the disadvantages of the definition of any abstraction as an unbounded or dynamic type. Prior to declaring a sequence the programmer should always carefully consider whether it is necessary to do so. If there is an acceptably low upper bound on the length (number of items) of the 'sequence' then an array declaration might well be preferable. Thus instead of

   s : **sequence of** item

we can very often use

   s : **array** [0 . . max] **of** item

The random access nature of arrays makes all sequence accessing operations efficient. Of course the drawback to substituting array declarations is their unsuitability for representing truly dynamic structures.

9.2 OPERATIONS ON SEQUENCES

Sequences are primarily only suitable for sequential processing. Usually processing in one direction is adequate, especially since two-way processing normally requires a somewhat more complex implementation. There is no generally acceptable set of sequence operations, the choice depends on the requirements of the application and to a lesser extent the properties of the implementation. However, a general set can be obtained from the two recursive type definitions, by treating them as normal records with fields that can be accessed and updated. These are denoted in the conventional manner.

s.tag
s.first
s.finalpart
s.last
s.initialpart

where s is some sequence type variable

s: **sequence of** item

Thus if s is the sequence

$$(v_1 \ v_2 \ v_3 \ldots v_{n-1} \ v_n)$$

then

s.tag = nonempty
s.first = v_1
s.finalpart = $(v_2 \ v_3 \ldots v_{n-1} \ v_n)$
s.last = v_n
s.initialpart = $(v_1 \ v_2 \ v_3 \ldots v_{n-1})$

The initialisation of s to an empty sequence is denoted by

s.init

When processing sequences we need to be able to identify individual items and subsequences. This can be achieved by the use of pointers to sequences.

p :↑ **sequence of** item

A pointer, p, may be dynamically bound to a particular sequence, s, by use of the operator @. Thus

$$p := @(s)$$

makes p point at the sequence s. (See figure 9.4.)

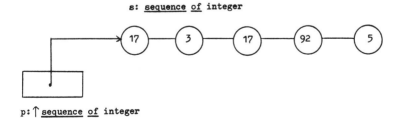

Figure 9.4 $p := @(s)$ *where* $s = (17\ 3\ 17\ 92\ 5)$

The components of 'where p points' may be accessed as for standard record structures. Thus if s and p have the values shown in figure 9.4 then

$p \uparrow$ .tag = nonempty
$p \uparrow$ .first = 17
$p \uparrow$ .finalpart = (3 17 92 5)
$p \uparrow$ .last = 5
$p \uparrow$ .initialpart = (17 3 17 92)

The instruction $p := @(p \uparrow$ .finalpart) causes p to move to the right one item, as shown in figure 9.5.

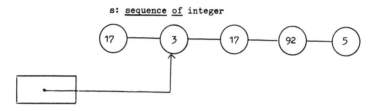

s: <u>sequence of</u> integer

p:↑ <u>sequence of</u> integer

Figure 9.5 The effect of the instruction sequence
$$p := @(s)$$
$$p := @(p \uparrow \text{.finalpart})$$
is to leave $p \uparrow = (3\ 17\ 92\ 5)$

We may search for a target item in either front-to-end, or end-to-front direction

```
var s : sequence of item;
        p :↑ sequence of item;
        target : item;
        found : boolean;
begin
{front-to-end search}
found := false;
p := @(s);
while p ↑ .tag = nonempty and not found
        do begin
            found := p ↑ .first = target;
            p := @(p ↑ .finalpart)
            end;
if found then . . .
    .
    :
    .
end
```

or in the reverse direction

```
begin
{end-to-front search}
found := false;
p := @(s);
while p ↑ .tag = nonempty and not found
      do begin
            found := p ↑ .last = target;
            p := @(p ↑ .initialpart)
         end;

if found then . . .
      .
      .
      .
end
```

It is important to realise that the use of pointers to sequences does not imply that the sequence structure is necessarily implemented using a linked structure. Pointers to sequences should be thought of as the computational analogue of using blackboard pointers during a lecture on sequences (figure 9.6). They are used to indicate which sequence is being referred to; they say nothing about how the sequence is drawn (implemented).

Figure 9.6 A lecture on sequences

The basic updating operations are the addition or deletion of single items at either the front or end of the sequence. These we denote by

$s.\text{addfront}(v)$ ⎫
$s.\text{addend}(v)$ ⎬   update s by adding a new item v to its ⎰front⎱ ⎱end⎰

$s.\text{deletefirst}$ ⎫
$s.\text{deletelast}$ ⎬   update the sequences by deleting the ⎰first⎱ ⎱last⎰ item; has no effect if $s.\text{tag} = \text{empty}$

These operations can be used to provide an assignment or copy operation

```
function assign(b :↑ sequence of item) :↑ sequence of item;
        {returns a pointer to a copy of sequence b}
        var p: ↑ sequence of item;
        begin
        p ↑ .init;
        while b ↑ .tag = nonempty
                do begin
                        p ↑ .addend(b ↑ .first);
                        b := @(b ↑ .finalpart)
                        end;

        assign := p
        end;
```

This function illustrates an important point about the specification of procedures that have structured objects as parameters. The semantics of value or input parameters requires that the entire structure be copied into the scope of the procedure. Apart from the circularity involved in the particular case of the assign operation, this is inefficient in both time and space. Consequently it is better to share the instance of the structured parameter by means of a pointer. Particular care must be taken when writing such procedures to ensure that they do not update the input structure, since this may cause the unpleasant side-effects associated with simultaneous value sharing and updating.

We conclude this section by solving a typical problem involving sequences.

Example

Design a program to perform the symbolic addition of two algebraic polynomials. For example, if polynomial a has the value

$$5x^7y^3 - 2x^3y^2 + 3xy + 5$$

and polynomial b has the value

$$6x^7y^3 + 4x^6y - 3xy + y - 1$$

then the result is

$$11x^7y^3 + 4x^6y - 2x^3y^2 + y + 4$$

The type polynomial can be defined as

type polynomial = **sequence of** term

where

```
term = record
        coeff : integer
        exponents : exponentype
        end
```

and

    exponentype = **record**
                  *x*exp,*y*exp : integer
                  end

The processing is simplified if for each polynomial, the terms are sorted in order of exponent. We have chosen to order sequences in descending order of exponents with the *x*-exponent taking precedence over the *y*-exponent. The ordering serves to facilitate the testing of whether a term with a given exponent value occurs in one, two or neither of the operand polynomials. The data files in the stock-update example of chapter 5 were ordered for a similar reason; using the reasoning behind that example we can formulate polynomial addition directly

    procedure polyaddition(*a, b* :↑ polynomial; **var** result :↑ polynomial);
        {symbolically adds polynomial *a*, to *b*, leaving result in result, all
        polynomials are sorted in descending order of exponent}
        var newterm : term;
        begin
        result ↑ .init;
        while (*a* ↑ .tag = nonempty **or** *b* ↑ .tag = nonempty)
            do begin
                if *a* ↑ .tag = empty **or**
                a ↑ .exponents ⊘ *b* ↑ .exponents   (i)
                then begin {the current *b* term is not in *a*}
                        result ↑ .addend (*b* ↑ .first)
                        b := @(*b* ↑ .finalpart)
                        end
                else if *b* ↑ .tag = empty **or**
                        b ↑ .exponents ⊘ *a* ↑ .exponents   (ii)
                        then begin {the current *a* term is not in *b*}
                                result ↑ .addend(*a* ↑ .first);
                                a := @(*a* ↑ .finalpart)
                                end
                else begin {current *a* and *b* terms have equal exponents}
                        newterm.coeff := *a* ↑ .coeff + *b* ↑ .coeff;
                        newterm.exponents := *a* ↑ .exponents;
                        if newterm.coeff ≠ 0 **then** {create new non-zero result term}
                                result ↑ .addend newterm;
                        a := @(*a* ↑ .finalpart);   {get next *a* term}
                        b := @(*b* ↑ .finalpart)   {get next *b* term}
                        end
            end;
        {have processed all the terms in polynomial *a* and *b*}
        end {of polyaddition}.

Lines (*i*), (*ii*): the operator ⊘ is 'less than' extended to cover the record type exponentype; it is defined to be false if either $a \uparrow$ .tag = empty or $b \uparrow$ .tag = empty.

From this algorithm we can see that for polynomial addition we need an implementation that supports the operations to access the tag, first and finalpart components of a sequence and in addition supports the operation addend. Hence when programming this algorithm we may use an implementation that optimises these sequence operations at the expense of all others.

9.3 STORAGE STRUCTURES FOR SEQUENCES

The basic model for implementing sequences is the linear linked list, but since the pointers all point in the same direction they are only suitable for one-way processing. The operations on a list variable s

> $s \uparrow$ .value,
> $s \uparrow$ .link,
> s = nil,

corresponds to the operations

> s.first,
> s.finalpart,
> s.tag = empty.

on a sequence variable s. Addition and deletion of items at the front of the sequence are provided by the list procedures addfront and deletefront given in section 8.5.

Addition can be generalised to insertion of a new item *after* the item designated by a pointer p.

Thus the operation insertafter (x, p) updates a sequence from that shown in figure 9.7 to that shown in figure 9.8.

It can be simply implemented by

```
procedure insertafter(i : itemtype; p :↑ node);
{insert new item i after item p ↑}
var t :↑ node;
begin {p must be ≠ nil}
t := free.acquire;
t ↑ .value := i;
t ↑ .link := p ↑ .link;
p ↑ .link := t
end
```

The effect of this procedure can be visualised as shown in figure 9.9.

If insertion before $p \uparrow$ is required then a pointer to the predecessor of $p \uparrow$ would seem necessary. However, a trick can be used which makes this

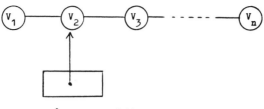

p: ↑ <u>sequence</u> <u>of</u> item

Figure 9.7

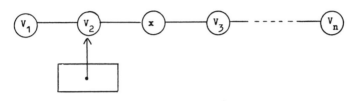

p: ↑ <u>sequence</u> <u>of</u> item

Figure 9.8 The effect of insertafter (x, p)

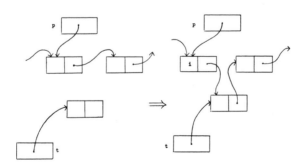

Figure 9.9

unnecessary. The insertion is made after p ↑ and then the values of the new item and p ↑ are interchanged, and finally p is moved on to the next item (figure 9.10).

Deletion of the item after pointer p is similarly quite simple

$t := p$ ↑ .link ;
p ↑ .link $:= t$ ↑ .link ;
free.return(t)

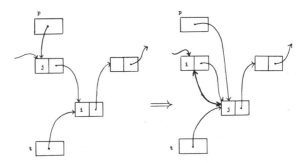

Figure 9.10 Insertion before p

Deleting the item $p\uparrow$.value itself can be achieved by copying the value of the successor node backwards into $p\uparrow$.value and then deleting the successor. It can only be applied when $p\uparrow$ has a successor, that is, $p\uparrow$ is not the last node on the list. The inclusion of a special end of list marker node can ensure this.

In some applications it is important to be able to access all the items of a sequence starting from an arbitrary one. This is done efficiently by making the lists circular. A circular list has the property that its last node links back to its first. The situation in figure 9.11 is typical.

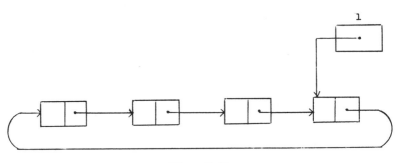

Figure 9.11

It is usual to consider that the sequence item, $l\uparrow$.value, is the last one, since in this way we also have ready access to the first item ($l\uparrow$.link$\uparrow$.value).

To simplify the processing of circular lists a special marker node may be included to mark their front. Such marker nodes only mark a position in the sequence, they do not contribute to the sequence value. The empty sequence value is as shown in figure 9.12 and a sequence with three items (1 2 3) would be represented as shown in figure 9.13.

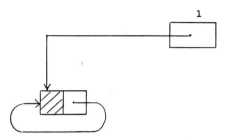

Figure 9.12

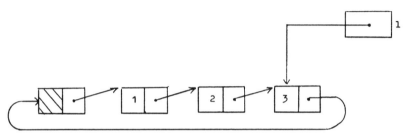

Figure 9.13

Apart from the simplicity of traversing an entire sequence, circular lists also allow the efficient implementation of adding an item to the end of a sequence.

```
procedure addend (i : integer);
var t :↑ node;      {auxiliary ptr}
begin
free.acquire(t);
t ↑ .value := i  ;
t ↑ .link  := l ↑ .link ;   {chain in new node}
l ↑ .link  := t  ;
l          := t  ;          {reset l}
end
```

When the two-way processing of sequences is required the usual solution is to use two-way linked lists as the storage structure. In two-way lists each node contains a sequence item and two pointers, one pointing to the preceding node and one pointing to the succeeding node (figure 9.14).

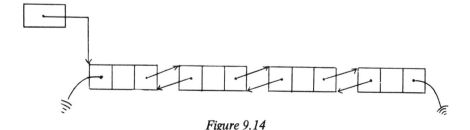

Figure 9.14

The reservoir for two-way lists can be implemented as for linear lists; only one pointer field needs to be used in the construction of the free-list.

The double links allow the deletion of the node designated by a pointer, p, itself, without recourse to tricks or to a 'trailing pointer' to keep track of the preceding node. The instruction sequence

$p \uparrow$ .left $\uparrow$ .right $:= p \uparrow$ .right;
$p \uparrow$ .right $\uparrow$ .left $:= p \uparrow$ .left

is sufficient, though the first and last nodes need slightly different handling since they have either no left, or no right, neighbour.

Two-way lists may be given a circular structure if two-way circular processing of sequences is desired (figure 9.15).

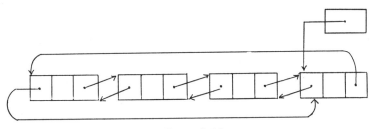

Figure 9.15

A disadvantage of any linked storage method is the amount of store required for the pointers and the time overheads of the store management system. This can become acute if the number of items in the sequence is large and the size of each item is small. In this situation, blocking — a combination of linked and contiguous methods — is practicable. The information from a number of nodes is stored consecutively in a fixed size block, the blocks are linked together using any of the standard methods. The packing density (items per block) determines the behavioural characteristics of blocked lists. The lower the density the more like pure lists they become; the higher the density the more they adopt the characteristics of contiguous implementations. By adopting a common block size for all lists we may make lists with different sized nodes share the same reservoir, thereby overcoming a serious drawback of linked storage structures — the need to supply a different reservoir for each size of node.

9.4 QUEUES

In many applications, the full generality of sequences is not required. Two particularly frequent forms of restricted sequence are known as *queues* and *stacks*. A *queue* is a sequence where all the additions occur at the end of the sequence and all the deletions and accesses occur at the front. A *stack* is a sequence where all the operations operate on the same end (either front or back). Because of their intimate connection with the implementation of recursion, stacks will be dealt with in chapter 12.

Queues occur frequently in operating systems. An operating system is a special program that is designed to make the use of computer hardware more convenient and efficient. Few programs can actually make full and simultaneous use of all the hardware resources of a computer. Therefore the unit costs of executing programs can be lowered by permitting the simultaneous execution of a number of programs. For the purposes of this discussion it matters little whether these programs are totally independent of each other or whether they are components of the operating system itself. The essential point is that a single processor unit is made to look like many processors by being switched from the execution of one program to another. This is known as the *time-sharing* of a hardware resource (the processor) among a number of consumer processes, where a process is an activity, namely the execution of a program by a processor. A saving is possible because the execution of any one program has to be suspended from time to time while it awaits the completion of a data transfer to or from a peripheral. During the period of suspension another process may proceed. The nucleus of an operating system is therefore concerned with organising the time-sharing of the processor, and the other similar resources such as disc input—output channels, and the operator's console. For each such time-shared resource the operating system nucleus has to maintain a *queue* of processes (a record of the current state of the execution of a program) ready and able to use the resource. As a process wishes to use a resource it joins the end of the queue, while the resource takes its next customer process from the front of the queue. In this way the resource takes its customers in the time order of their requests, although by reordering the queue it is simple to implement a priority scheme. Most operating systems allow only a relatively few and constant number of processes, consequently each queue can only ever be short. The execution time of the queue operations must be minimal because they determine the cost of process switching. Since process switching can occur in the order of every 10 or 20 ms, the efficiency of the queue operations clearly influences the operating system's ability to respond to real time events and its over-all efficiency. The usual implementation is therefore to use circularly linked lists, with two-way pointers if any priority reordering is necessary. If there is a fixed number of processes in the system then there is no need for a store management system.

Queues are also useful as a means of allowing two asynchronous and parallel processes to communicate with each other. A producing process A may communicate with a consuming process B by placing items (or 'messages') into a queue from which process B takes items (figure 9.16).

If either the consumer or producer process is the activity of a peripheral device then the queue is commonly known as a buffer. The number of items in the queue at any point in time depends on the relative rates of production and consumption. The queue serves to even out the fluctuations in supply and demand; but it can only succeed in this task if, measured over some period of time, the two rates are equal. If consumption consistently outstrips production

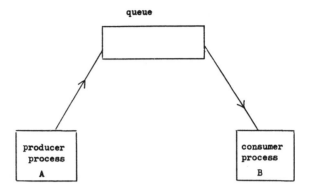

Figure 9.16

then the queue will shrink until it becomes empty, at which point the consumer process must be suspended until the producer can catch up. Similarly if production consistently outstrips consumption, then the queue will grow indefinitely, unless, as a precaution, an upper bound is placed on the queue length so that the producer is suspended once this limit is reached. Thus the buffer entry procedures also serve to synchronise the two processes. Because they are bounded, buffer queues are normally implemented using arrays

```
type queue of item =
class     {bounded queue or buffer of size n}
var b : array [0 .. n − 1] of item;
      count : integer;     {range 0 .. n}
      last : 0 .. n − 1;   {position of last entry}
procedure entry enter (x : item);
      begin
      if count = n then suspend producer process;   {queue full}        (i)
      b [last]  := x;
      last := last ⊕ 1;                                                  (ii)
      count := count + 1;
      release consumer process;     {if one is suspended because
                                          of empty queue}                (iii)
      end;
procedure entry get (var x : item);
      begin
      if count = 0 then suspend consumer process   {queue empty};   (iv)
      x := b [last ⊖ count] ;                                        (v)
      count :=  count − 1;
      release producer process;   {if one is suspended of queue full}  (vi)
      end;
function entry empty : boolean;
      begin
      empty := (count = 0);
      end;
```

```
function entry full : boolean;
    begin
    full := (count = n),
    end;
begin
count := 0; last := 0
end
```

Lines (i), (iii), (iv), (vi): (process synchronisation) if the queue is full on an enter operation then the producer must be *suspended* until a get operation (see line vi). Likewise if the queue is empty on a get operation the consumer must be suspended until an enter operation (see line iii). *Lines (ii), (v)*: $\oplus$, $\ominus$ indicates addition and subtraction modulon, to enable the in-use portion of b to wrap-around.

Details of how processes may be *suspended* and *released* depend on the operating system or hardware in use and need not concern us. One further precaution must be taken if the queue is to operate properly and that is to ensure that the get and enter operations cannot be activated simultaneously by the parallel processes, since this could lead to corruption of last, count, etc. In some cases runtime checking is unnecessary since the context guarantees that simultaneous activation is impossible. Where this cannot be guaranteed a runtime check (for example, switching off the interrupt system) must be implemented. Classes which control the synchronisation of processes and therefore need runtime checks to prevent simultaneous access of the class procedures are known as *monitors*. A discussion of monitors lies outside the scope of this book but the reader is referred to the excellent papers of Hoare (1974) and Brinch Hansen (1975a).

9.5 SUMMARY

1. A sequence is a dynamic structure whose elements are subject to a linear ordering. Sequences have a recursive definition.
2. Their basic method of implementation is the linear linked list, although there is a number of more sophisticated variations.
3. A queue is a sequence where all the additions occur at the end of the sequence, and all deletions and accesses occur at the front.

9.6 BIBLIOGRAPHICAL NOTES

Section 9.1, on recursive type definitions is based on 'Recursive Data Structures' (Hoare, 1975) and the exercises at the end of chapter 4 in Wirth (1975). The relationship between the Kleene star operation and right linear grammars can be found in most standard works on formal language theory, for example, Hopcroft and Ullman (1969). The discussion of sequences is a modification of that contained in 'Notes on Data Structuring' (Hoare, 1972b). The implementation of sequences is described fully in Knuth (1968). Madnick (1967) contains a survey of methods of implementing character strings.

The use of scheduler queues is a standard technique covered in books on operating systems, for example, Lister (1975). The discussion of bounded buffer queues is based on the monitor concept (Hoare, 1974 and Brinch Hansen, 1975a). *Operating System Principles* (Brinch Hansen, 1973) is an excellent account of structured programming applied to operating systems, though it slightly predates the development of monitors and classes. The SOLO system (Brinch Hansen, 1976) is the first example of an operating system to utilise these techniques.

Exercises 2

2.1 Design an abstract algorithm to make a copy of a sequence with the order of the items reversed. Refine this algorithm for the cases where the sequence is implemented as (a) a linear linked list and (b) a circularly linked list.

2.2 The algorithm for finding the reachable set of a given node in a graph (section 6.3) is inefficient because it unnecessarily re-evaluates, on every iteration, the set of nodes directly reachable from every node in the reachable set. Modify the algorithm so that only the nodes directly reachable from the new, and previously unreached nodes, are evaluated on each iteration.

2.3 Design a set of library routines for polynomial arithmetic by designing abstract algorithms for subtraction, multiplication and division. (Consider the coefficient of each term to be of type real rather than integer.) Specify a suitable storage structure for the type polynomial.

2.4 Write a simple scanning algorithm for the substring testing operation

    function includes (s, p : string) : boolean

which returns true if the character string s contains the string p as a substring and false otherwise. Estimate the computational cost of your algorithm as a function of the lengths of s and p.

2.5 The basic substring testing algorithm (exercise 2.4) can be improved by a number of simple modifications

(a) cease scanning if length (p) is greater than the remaining length of s
(b) check the first and last characters of s before checking those in between.

Modify the algorithm developed in exercise 2.4 and specify the desirable characteristics of a string implementation from the viewpoint of this operation, substring testing.

2.6 Design a complete set of library routines for string processing. Specify a suitable implementation on a 16-bit word minicomputer.

2.7 (Jackson, 1975) Devise a solution to the following problem using two concurrent processes and a bounded buffer as the means of intercommunication. You may assume that as one process is putting an item into the buffer the other getting process is automatically locked out and vice versa.

An input file on paper tape contains the text of a number of telegrams. The tape is accessed by a read block instruction which reads, into an array of characters, a variable length string of characters terminated by an end of block 'eob' character. A block cannot exceed 100 characters excluding the 'eob' character. Each block contains a number of words separated by one or more space characters. Zero or more space characters may precede the first word and follow the last word in the block. The tape is terminated by an end of file block whose first character is 'eof'.

Each telegram consists of a number of words terminated by the special word 'ZZZZ'. The last telegram is followed by a null telegram consisting only of 'ZZZZ'.

The output from the program is to be an analysis of the telegram consisting of a header line 'Telegram analysis' followed by a two-line report for each telegram consisting of

'Telegram number i'
'w words of which n are oversize'

where w is the total number of words in the telegram and n is the number of words exceeding 12 characters in length. The output is terminated by the line 'end of analysis'.

2.8 The type integer may be considered to be defined by

type integer = **sequence of** digit

thus allowing completely variable length arithmetic. Using this definition design a variable length integer arithmetic package.

2.9 An efficient implementation of the variable length arithmetic package (exercise 2.8) should use some form of linked list structure in which the values at each node are of type 'hardware integer'. Apart from requiring less space, this allows the use of the hardware arithmetic functions, thus saving time. Develop and modify your answer to exercise 2.8 to take this into account, bearing in mind that some arithmetic operations can give double length results.

2.10 If a sequence suffers relatively few dynamic changes it may be represented by a compact list in which the items are stored as contiguous nodes unless an explicit link node indicates otherwise. For example, the sequence $(v_1, v_2, v_3, v_4, v_5, v_6)$ might be stored as shown in the figure, where v indicates a value node and l indicates a link node.

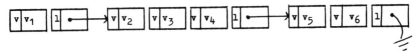

Figure Exercise 2.10

(a) What are the advantages of such a representation for sequences?
(b) How might storage management be handled for this representation?
(c) Implement the following sequence operations using this representation (i) a 'front-to-end' search, (ii) addfront and deletefirst, (iii) assignment by copying.

10 *Simple Searching Techniques*

10.1 SPARSE MAPPINGS

For a mapping or function to be represented by an array it is necessary that the domain type be both finite and of small enough cardinality to allow the allocation of a unique part of store for each array element. Likewise set structures, which have a small enough base type, are capable of an efficient bitstring representation in which an individual bit is allocated to each possible set element. Exceeding the restriction, as in the case of integer sets, necessitates an altogether different representation. However, in many applications the programmer cannot avoid requiring a structure representation for a function with large or infinite domain or for a set with large or infinite base type. A structural representation is only possible for sets that have only a small number of domain elements and for functions that map only a few values into significant range values. By 'significant' we mean differing from a specified null or default value. Such structures are known as **sparse** sets and arrays

> **type** S = **sparse set of** T
> **type** A = **sparse array** D **of** R

The sparse set type S is essentially a special case of the sparse array in which the base type is mapped in to type boolean, that is

> **type** S = **sparse array** T **of** boolean

Sparse structures frequently arise in a data processing context where large amounts of data are common. In a payroll program, for example, a table mapping employee works numbers into employee details might be declared as a

> **sparse array** worksnumber **of** employeedetails

because works numbers are often six- or eight-character alphanumeric types even when there are only a few hundred employees. Similar considerations would lead to the flight passenger list in an airline booking program to be declared as

> passengerlist : **sparse set of** ticketnumbers

Sparse structures frequently arise in all areas of programming and are indeed absolutely central to many scientific data processing applications.

We may also regard sparse arrays as the static representation of a *partial* function rather than a total function between the domain and range, that is, a function which is only defined for some of the domain values, the others having the default value 'undefined'. This view is often the appropriate one in commercial data processing applications, for example, the table mentioned above

> **sparse array** worksnumber **of** employeedetails

specifies a function which is only defined for certain works number values.

10.2 SPARSITY AND SEARCHING

Because sparse sets are a particular case of sparse arrays, we may treat the implementation of sparse sets and arrays together. The basis of all methods is to store only those elements that are significant, a single default value being stored separately if required. When the number of significant elements varies greatly at runtime then they must be organised in a dynamic data structure. Updating or accessing a sparse structure consequently necessitates a search of the directory of significant values for a target domain value. In the implementation of

> **sparse array** D **of** R

the directory must contain an entry for each significant value

> **type** entry = **record**
>   key : D;
>   info : R
>   **end**

Each entry maps a domain value, in the key field, into the corresponding range value held in the info field. If multi-dimensional sparse arrays are to be implemented then the key field of the entry can be made a record type. For example

> **sparse array** $[i \, . \, . \, m, j \, . \, . \, n]$ **of** R

requires entries of type

> **record**
> key : **record**
>   sub1 : $i \, . \, . \, m$;
>   sub2 : $j \, . \, . \, n$
>   **end**;
> info : R
> **end**

Because this representation flattens the array it can result in traversals on one subscript being efficient but traversals on the others being less so. No info field is necessary in the case of sparse sets, since the presence of a key is sufficient to show that the key is a member of the set.

In choosing a storage structure the primary criterion is: does it support an efficient search method? One other important consideration is whether the variation in the number of significant values necessitates a dynamic data structure.

In other words when the number of significant values is essentially static we treat the declaration of

sparse array D **of** R

as if it were

record
directory : **array** $[1 .. \max]$ **of** entry;
size   : $0 .. \max$;   {no significant entries}
default : R
end

whereas when it is dynamic the declaration is considered as

record
directory : **sequence of** entry;
size   : integer;   {no of significant entries}
default : R
end

or some other dynamic data structure.

Searching techniques may be classified as

(1) controlled scan: the directory entries are accessed in a systematic and preplanned fashion until a match is found or the entire directory has been searched; or
(2) hashing (or key transformation): each entry is stored at a position in the directory which related to its key value and the composition of the directory at the time of the insertion.

Controlled scan techniques, especially as applied to static directories, are the simplest and hence we shall consider them first. Other search techniques will be considered in chapters 11 and 13.

10.3 LINEAR SEARCH

The linear search is the most straightforward and simple of the controlled scan search techniques. It consists simply of starting at some directory entry, usually the first, and comparing each entry key with the target key, one at a time, until either a match is found or all the directory positions have been searched. This is, of course, the method we have used in the implementation of function has, etc., for integersets. Recalling previous discussions we can see that linear searching is equally applicable to array and to sequence implementations.

To compare various search methods a quantitative measure of their efficiency, known as average search length, is used. The *average search length* A_p of some search technique p is defined by

$$A_p = \frac{1}{n} \sum_{i=1}^{n} s_i$$

where n is the number of significant directory entries and s_i is the average number of comparisons required to locate the ith entry.

For the linear search method

$$s_i = i$$

as the first entry will be located on the first comparison, the second entry on the second comparison, etc. Therefore

$$A_{\text{linearsearch}} = \frac{1}{n} \sum_{i=1}^{n} i$$

$$= \frac{n+1}{2}$$

In other words the efficiency of a linear search is proportional to the number of directory entries; as we shall see this can be improved quite considerably by other techniques.

The assumption behind average search length is that the distribution of target keys is random; if this is not the case significant improvements can be achieved by storing the most frequently required target keys at the front of the directory. This is only done at the expense of keeping the directory in a particular order and consequently this variation is normally only worth while if the directory is static and unchanging.

Whatever target is being sought a linear search can only be declared unsuccessful after the whole directory has been examined, thus an unsuccessful search always requires n probes.

The coding of a linear search algorithm conventionally requires two tests per iteration, one to check for a match and one to check for having finished examining all the significant entries in the directory

```
type entry = record
              key : domain;
              info : range
              end
```

```
var directory : array [1 .. n] of entry;
    size        : 0 .. n;   {number of significant entries}
    i           : integer;
    found       : boolean;
begin
   .
   .
   .
found := false;
i := 1;
while i ⩽ size and not found
       do if directory [i] .key = target
            then found := true
            else i := i + 1;
if found then    {target found at position i}
       else    {not in directory}
   .
   .
   .
end
```

At the slight inconvenience of always keeping an entry of the directory available, the search can be performed with only one test per iteration. The target is merely inserted at the end of directory to act as a sentinel

```
var size : 0 .. n − 1;   {always keep one position empty}
begin
directory [size + 1] .key := target;    {insert sentinel to ensure
                                          termination of search}

i := 1;
while directory [i] .key ≠ target do i := i + 1;
if i ≠ size + 1 then    {target found at position i}
              else    {not in directory}
   .
   .
   .
end
```

This coding trick can be used whenever the implementation allows insertion at the end of the directory.

Linear searching is unsophisticated but of practical use where a directory has few entries. Unlike other methods it does not depend on the directory being sorted in any particular order, and hence it is often used to advantage in conjunction with other techniques.

10.4 MERGE SEARCH

In many applications a program has to deal with a series of target values one after the other. The total computational effort in searching for the target values can be significantly reduced if they are processed in ascending (or descending) order and the directory is maintained in the same order. The keys are compared starting with the first directory entry and the first target. If a match is not found, the directory is scanned until an equal or greater key is found. If greater, the directory does not have an entry with the target key; if equal the target is in the directory. The next target value can be processed from the following directory without starting from position one. The merge search technique was used in the master-update example of chapter 5 and the polynomial addition example of chapter 9.

The major overhead of merge searching is the cost of arranging for the series of target values to be used in the correct order *vis-à-vis* the directory. If the target values are stored as data then they must be sorted, but sometimes, as in the case of integers, they can be generated in the correct order by some simple algorithmic enumeration of the domain type. This is often possible in the case of sparse vectors or matrices, since most operations necessitate a systematic traversal of the matrix. In the case of matrices with two or more dimensions it is possible to deal with the dimensions in a symmetric fashion, thus permitting traversals on all the dimensions to be done with equal efficiency. The method is based on the circular linked list implementation of sequences. Consider two-dimensional arrays of the type

array $[D_1, D_2]$ **of** R

In this implementation each actually used value of D_1 is placed in one circular list and each actually used value of D_2 is placed in another. These are the so-called border chains. Each node of either border chain points to a circular linked list of nodes containing the elements which have the same subscript. The final node points back to the appropriate border chain entry. Each non-default array element is represented by a node containing the subscript and range values, a pointer to the next node with the same D_1 subscript, and a pointer to the next node with the same D_2 subscript. Thus each non-default element may be pictured as being on the intersection of the lines of a two-dimensional grid, with pointers leading across and downwards to the next non-default element on the same row or column. (See figure 10.1.)

A row by row traversal is performed by successively locating the appropriate border chain row entry and doing a merge search on the row entries. Column by column traversals are performed similarly.

In general the merge search technique is highly efficient for the processing of target values which are naturally in order. The cost of maintaining a sorted directory is also minimal as long as all insertions and removals are performed sequentially. The other advantage of merge searching is that because it is sequential, only one target value and one directory entry need be available together and therefore it is particularly suitable for use with sequential files.

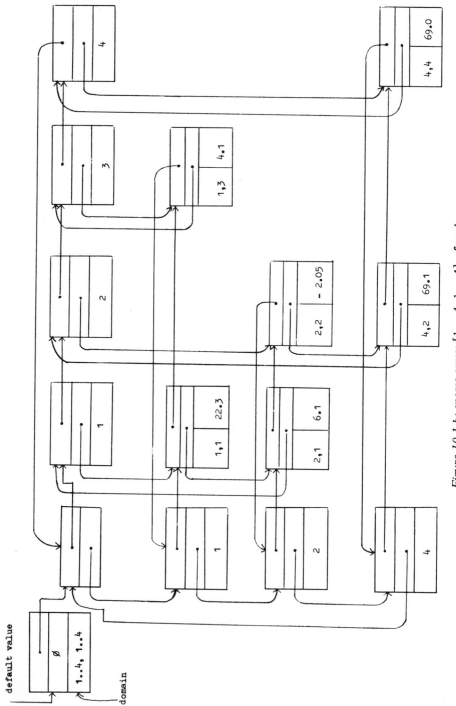

Figure 10.1 b: sparse array $[1 . . 4, 1 . . 4]$ of real

10.5 BINARY SEARCH

Binary searching is a fundamental technique of programming. For a random distribution of target values it makes the most effective use possible of the ordering of entries in a sorted directory. Let $d = (e_1, e_2, \ldots, e_n)$ be a directory sorted in ascending order on the key fields of each entry e_i; if the middle† entry e_k, say, is accessed and compared with the target key then three possibilities exist.

(1) e_k.key < target   the keys of all the entries to the left of e_k are less than e_k.key and hence a further search should be restricted to that part of the directory which is to the right of e_k

(2) e_k.key > target   for analogous reasons a further search should be restricted to the entries to the left of e_k

(3) e_k.key = target   the desired entry is located.

Repeatedly bisecting and testing in this way will either (a) find an entry with the target key value or (b) reduce the area to be searched to zero if the entry is not in the directory.

It is not essential to extract the middle key for the search process to work, but it is more efficient, bcause by bisecting we are ensuring that wherever the target lies the two remaining areas that might have to be searched are of the same size.

The following abstract program describes binary searching more formally; the operations middle, leftpart, rightpart and empty have their intuitive meaning and ← denotes assignment by value sharing.

```
begin
searcharea ← directory;    {set the searcharea to cover the whole directory}
found := false
while not found and not searcharea empty
        do if searcharea.middle < target
              then searcharea.rightpart
            else if searcharea.middle > target
              then searcharea.leftpart
            else found := true;
    {either found = true and searcharea.middle = target
    or     found = false and target is not in the directory}
end
```

If the directory is static then the random accessing nature of arrays provides a simple implementation of the necessary operations.

```
var directory    : array [1 .. n] of entry;
    size         : integer;    {range 0 .. n}
    lower, upper : integer;    {limits of searcharea}
    found        : boolean;
```

† If n is even then the middle element may be taken as either (n **div** 2) or ((n **div** 2) + 1).

```
begin
lower := 1; upper := size;    {searcharea covers the significant portion of
                                                            directory}
found := false;
while not found and lower ⩽ upper
      do begin
            middle := (lower + upper) div 2;
            if target > directory [middle] .key
               then lower := middle + 1
            else if target < directory [middle] .key
                  then upper := middle − 1
            else found := true
            end;
   if found then    {target = directory [middle] .key}
           else     {target is not in directory}
end
```

The algorithm works by ensuring that at the start of each iteration

$$\text{directory}[k] \text{ .key} < \text{target for } k = 1 \ldots \text{low} - 1$$

and

$$\text{directory}[k] \text{ .key} > \text{target for } k = \text{upper} + 1 \ldots \text{size}$$

(See figure 10.2.) The target must be in the shaded area iff it is in the directory and each iteration reduces the size of the shaded area.

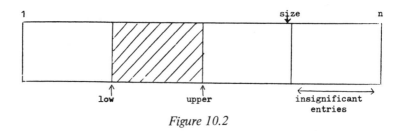

Figure 10.2

Dynamic directories can be processed using the binary search method but a linking technique more sophisticated than linear linked lists is required. The necessary techniques will be dealt with in chapter 13.

10.6 PROPERTIES OF BINARY SEARCHING

Consider a sorted directory, with 15 entries whose keys are k_1 to k_{15}. The first comparison of a binary search will be with k_8; the second comparisons (if necessary) will be with either k_4 or k_{12}; the third comparisons will be with k_2, k_6, k_{10} or k_{14}, and so on, until the target is found or all the keys have been eliminated. This process can be represented by a binary tree diagram in which a node, k_n, indicates the comparison with key k_n and the branches represent the comparison to be made next (figure 10.3).

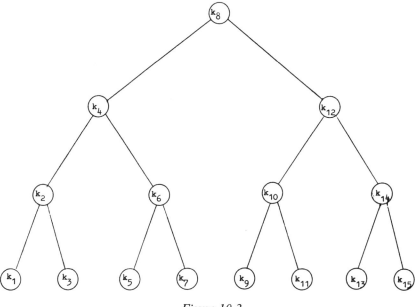

Figure 10.3

From this diagram it can be seen that the search for entry k_1 requires four probes whereas k_{12} requires only two and k_8 only one. In each case the number of comparisons is one greater than the length of the path from the root (k_8) to the node itself. The average search length is therefore the average of this value over all nodes on the binary decision tree for the directory.

$$\text{Average search length} = \frac{2^0 \times 1 + 2^1 \times 2 + 2^2 \times 3 + 2^3 \times 4}{15}$$

$$= \frac{49}{15}$$

$$= 3.263$$

The method of constructing binary decision trees can be applied to any directory, making it possible to prove the following result by induction on the directory size.

For a directory of size n and for some integer k such that $2^{k-1} < n < 2^k$, then

(1) a successful binary search requires a minimum of 1, maximum of k probes
(2) an unsuccessful binary search requires

k probes if $n = 2^{k-1}$
$k - 1$ or k probes if $2^{k-1} < n < (2^k - 1)$

A similar but more commonly known result, which requires more detailed analysis is that the average search length of a binary search is proportional to $\log_2 n$. Table 10.1 compares the values of $(n + 1)/2$ and $\log_2 n$ to illustrate the relative merits of binary searching *vis-à-vis* linear searching.

Table 10.1

Number of Significant Entries n	Linear Searching $(n + 1)/2$	Binary Searching $\log_2 n$
5	3.0	2.3
10	5.5	3.3
50	25.5	5.6
100	50.5	6.6
500	250.5	9.0
1000	500.5	9.9

A mitigating factor in favour of linear searching is the simplicity of the algorithm which leads to a reduced time per probe. Each iteration of the linear search requires one test and one increment, whereas the binary search requires at least three tests, one addition followed by a shift (division by 2) and one increment or decrement. In other words we may assume an advantage of the order of 5 to 1 in favour of linear searching, making the break-even point around a 50-entry directory.

The binary search overhead of initially sorting the directory is often negated by the inevitability of sorting due to a need to output a directory in a form readily processable by humans.

10.7 SUMMARY

1. An array mapping, $f: D \rightarrow R$, is known as sparse if D is a very large or infinite type but only a few domain elements are mapped into values differing from some specified default value.
2. A sparse set has a large or infinite base type but only a small number of elements.

3. Sparse mappings and sets can be represented by storing only those elements that are significant, and conducting a search whenever an access is required.
4. The average search length of a search technique A_p, is defined by

$$A_p = \frac{1}{n} \sum_{i=1}^{n} s_i$$

where n is the number of directory entries and s_i is the average number of comparisons required to locate the ith entry. Average search length is only a relevant measure of efficiency where the distribution of targets is random and all the searches are successful.
5. For a linear search, $A = (n + 1)/2$; however, it is a very flexible method.
6. The merge search is very efficient if targets always occur in either ascending or descending order.
7. For a binary search, average search length is proportional to $\log_2 n$.

10.8 BIBLIOGRAPHICAL NOTES

The treatment of sparse mappings is due to Hoare (1972b). The searching methods discussed in this chapter have been known since the earliest days of computer science and are dealt with in most books on programming. Knuth (1973) gives a comprehensive account of these methods.

11 *Hashing Techniques*

11.1 INTRODUCTION

Previously we have looked at the methods of implementing sparse mappings which conduct searches according to some preplanned scanning strategy. In this chapter we discuss a family of methods where the position of an entry in a directory is related to the value of its key; these methods are known as *hashing* techniques. Because hashing involves explicitly computing the position of an entry from its key, the technique is only applicable where there is fixed upper bound on the number of directory entries. Hashed directories will therefore be considered as array structures

> **array** $[0 .. n]$ **of** entry

though in essence it is immaterial whether the array is held in main store or on backing store as a randomly accessible file.

The basis of the technique is to use a many-to-one function — the *hashing* function — to map the key type into directory positions. For example, consider the sparse mapping formed by the symbol table of a compiler for a high-level language.

> symbol table : **sparse array** identifier **of** storeaddress

This is the classic application of hashing techniques. It requires a hashing function

> h : identifier $\rightarrow (0 .. n)$

like nametype

together with a directory

> directory : **array** $[0 .. n]$ **of** entry

where

> **type** entry = **record**
> > key : identifier;
> > info : storeaddress
> > **end**

Figure 11.1 shows a hashed symbol table.

position	key: identifier	info: storeaddress
h(NEXT)=0 0	NEXT	46
h(TOTAL)=2 1		
etc 2	TOTAL	57
	RESULT	23
.	NUMB	30
.		
.		
n	EMPTY	15

Figure 11.1 Hashed symbol table

Given an identifier k, we can locate its storeaddress by accessing

directory $[h(k)]$. info

However, since h is a many-to-one function it is possible to have two identifiers, k_1 and k_2, such that $k_1 \neq k_2$ but $h(k_1) = h(k_2)$. This will cause a problem when we attempt to insert a new entry with key k_2 and we find the table already contains an entry with key k_1. This situation is called a *collision* or *overflow*; the difference between the various hashing techniques is in the way they handle the collisions. (See figure 11.2.)

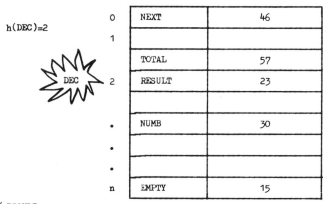

DEC $\not=$ RESULT,

but h(DEC) = h(RESULT) = 2

Figure 11.2 Hashed symbol table with collision

Our discussion of hashing techniques covers two aspects; what constitutes a good hashing function and how to handle collisions.

11.2 CHOICE OF A HASHING FUNCTION

A principal consideration in the choice of a hashing function is the avoidance of collisions. This can be achieved by selecting a function for which the range

(1)   is distributed evenly across the set of directory positions, and
(2)   is as random as possible, that is, is not dependent on any particular pattern in the keys.

It is from these two requirements that the name hashing derives to 'make a mess of' or to 'chop up' the argument. In addition it is essential that the function should be fast to evaluate on the computer to be used. A function involving division should be avoided on a machine without division hardware.

There are four principal techniques which may be used in combination.

(*i*) *Truncation*

This is one of the simplest methods in which part of the key is truncated and the part left is used for the directory position. The evaluation is fast though truncation frequently fails to give randomly distributed positions. For example, the key 377322, by truncating the last three digits would give the position 377. However, if the frequency of occurrence of keys starting with 37 is high, then there is a high probability of collisions. This method is usually used in combination with other methods.

(*ii*) *Folding*

In this method, the key is partitioned into several parts each of which, with the possible exception of the last one, has the same length as the directory position. These parts are then summed together to form the directory position. Information in all parts of the key therefore plays a part in forming the position. This overcomes the uneven distribution that occurs with truncation. The two keys 377322 and 377323 when folded in half produce the positions $377 + 322 = 699$ and $377 + 323 = 700$ whereas when truncated to the first three digits they both produce position 377.

(*iii*) *Multiplicative Methods*

Multiplicative methods generally perform better than the previous two methods with respect to a spread, but they increase overhead time. They consist of multiplying the key either by itself or by a constant and extracting any n-bit field to be the position; for example, the mid-square method consists of squaring the key and extracting the middle part from the result: if the key is 587, squaring would give $587 \times 587 = 344569$; the directory position is then 456.

(iv) Division

One of the best and most frequently used methods with respect to spread is to use a fixed-point division method, which consists of dividing the key word by the directory size and using the remainder as the position. To get even spread it is usual to make the directory size a prime number. Generally this method is slower than multiplicative methods but superior with respect to spread.

11.3 COLLISION HANDLING BY OPEN ADDRESSING

In this section we consider the class of hash techniques that locates overflow entries in open or empty positions in the directory. Naturally, the sequence of positions probed after a collision must always be the same for a given key. Thus for open addressing techniques there must be two functions: the hashing function

h : keytype $\rightarrow 0 \ldots n - 1$

which is used to find the initial directory position and an increment function

inc : keytype $\rightarrow 0 \ldots n - 1$

which is used to search the directory for an empty position in the event of a collision. It follows therefore that for every key, k, inc(k) should be relatively prime to n, so that the whole directory be searched.

Before considering possible choices for the increment function we shall consider the implementation of the sparse mapping

personnelfile : **sparse array** worksno **of** employeedetail

For the sake of simplicity, we assume that only two operations, retrieve and insert, are required on this type, the problems associated with deletion are considered later.

(1) personnelfile.retrieve(w) which is a function returning the employee details associated with works number w, if the mapping is defined for w. If it is not defined then a special employee details value 'undefined' is to be returned.

(2) personnelfile.insert(w,e,s) which associates the employee details value, e, with the works number w and returns the status value 'ok' in s. If there is insufficient room in the directory then the mapping is unaltered and s is returned with value 'fail'.

A class can be constructed to implement this mapping

```
type sparse array worksno of employeedetails =
class
const n = {size of directory};
type entry = record
         key : worksno;
         info: employeedetails
         end;
```

```
var directory : array [0 .. n − 1] of entry;
    i,p    : 0 .. n − 1;   {initial and subsequent probe position}
    found : boolean;
    emptyposn : boolean;
begin
function h(k : worksno) : 0 .. n − 1;
      {hashing function}                                              (i)
   end;
function inc(k : worksno) : 0 .. n − 1;                               (ii)
      {increment function}
end;
procedure locate (k : worksno);
      {local procedure to search for an entry with key = k}
   begin
   i := h(k); p := i;  {initial probe at i}
   found := false; emptyposn := false;
   repeat
         if directory [p] .key = k then found := true
         else if directory [p].key = empty then emptyposn := true     (iii)
            else p := p ⊖ inc(k)                                      (iv)
   until p = i or found or emptyposn;                                 (v)
   end;
function entry retrieve (k : worksno) : employeedetails;
   begin
   locate(k);
   if found then retrieve := directory [p].info
         else retrieve := undefined
   end;
procedure entry insert (k : worksno; e : employeedetails; var status :
                                                        (ok, fail));
   begin
   locate(k);
   status := ok;
   if found then {update an existing entry}
         directory [p].info := e
   else if directory [p].key = empty then {insert new entry}
                                       begin
                                       directory [p].key := k
                                       directory [p].info := e
                                       end
   else {p = i, directory is full}
         status := fail;
   end;
begin
      {initialise hashing and increment functions if necessary}
      for p = 0 to n − 1       {clear directory to empty}             (vi)
         do directory [p].key := empty;
end;
```

Line (i): the body of the hashing function is immaterial to open addressing methods. *Line (ii)*: different open addressing techniques are distinguished by different increment functions (see below). *Lines (iii), (vi)*: on initialisation the directory is cleared, to some null works number value 'empty', consequently when a position with an empty key is located the search may be terminated. *Line (iv)*: the operator $\ominus$ indicates modulo n subtraction; this is necessary to ensure that the whole directory is searched in the event of a collision. *Line (v)*: when $p = i$ we have searched the whole directory after a collision, this implies the directory is full.

If the value inc(k) is uniformly 1 for all key values then a linear search is performed for an empty position in the event of a collision. This is the simplest of the open addressing techniques and is known as *linear probing*. Consider two directory positions p_1, p_2, such that $p_2 = p_1 \ominus 1$, a collision at p_1 will cause a search through positions $p_1 \ominus 1, p_1 \ominus 2, \ldots, p_1 \oplus 1$ for an empty position. This compounds the probability of a collision at p_2 and subsequent positions and thus leads to a *clustering* of entries. Clustering seriously affects the average search time for linear probing.

At the expense of another hashing function, inc(k) can be a pseudo-random number function. *Random probing* avoids the problem of clustering but there is a number of more efficient methods that can be used.

This *quadratic-search* method is faster than the pseudo-random number method mentioned above, and yet avoids the problems raised by the linear probing method. In effect, after a collision at directory position p this method tries probes at $p + ai + bi^2$ (modulo n) for $i = 1, 2, 3, \ldots$, where a and b are constants, normally $+1$ or -1. When the directory size is a power of 2 the quadratic search is usually too small for effective use. But when the directory size is a prime a quadratic search always covers exactly half of the directory. This is entirely adequate for most purposes; in fact it is usual with this method to declare the directory full when the search fails after having looked at half the directory. The quadratic search is not affected by clustering. If the search passes over the hash addresses $p_1, p_2, p_3, \ldots, p_n$ when starting from p_1, then it will not pass over a sequence of elements $p_i, p_{i+1}, \ldots, p_n$ when starting from p_i, for $i > 1$.

The *linear quotient* method uses a single division to provide pseudo-random values for the hashing and increment functions

$h(k) = $ remainder (k/n)
inc(k) $= $ **if** quotient $(k/n) = 0$(modulo n) **then** 1 {inc(k) must be
made non-zero}
  else quotient (k/n)

where the directory size n must be a prime number.

Given hardware division the method is very fast; it probes the entire directory and does not suffer from clustering. It is therefore often the best open addressing technique.

Entries cannot be removed from an open hash address by simply marking the position as empty. A special 'deleted' value is required which indicates that the position may be filled on insertion but must not be used as a condition to terminate retrieval. Deleted space can thus be reclaimed but the search time is not shortened.

When linear probing is being used, it is possible, at the expense of some extra work, to delete entries in such a way that it avoids this sorry state of affairs. The deletion process need only search for, and move up, any entries, equivalent to the one to be deleted, that arrived after it. The validity of the algorithm depends on the fact that for linear probing inc(k) is independent of k; no analogous deletion procedure exists for use with the alternative open addressing techniques.

Using this method we may add a new procedure to the class

```
procedure entry remove (k : worksno);
        {deletes an entry with key = k, if one exists}
    begin
    locate(k);
    if found then begin {delete entry at position p}
            directory [p].key := empty;
            j := p ⊖ 1;                                              (i)
            while directory [j].key ≠ empty and j ≠ i do            (ii)
                begin
                if h(directory [j].key) = i                         (iii)
                    then begin {equivalent keys under h}
                            {shuffle down entry}
                            directory [p] := directory [j] ;
                            p := j;
                            directory [p].key := empty
                         end;
                j := j ⊖ 1;
                end
            end
    end;
```

Lines (*i*), (*iii*): as a result of locate(k), p = position of entry with k = key, i = initial probe = $h(k)$. *Line* (*ii*): terminate at end of 'cluster'.

11.4 ORDERED HASHING (Amble and Knuth, 1974)

In general the average search length of a hashing technique depends on the load factor (proportion of non-empty positions). But whatever the technique, an unsuccessful search will generally require more probes than a successful search. Successful termination occurs as soon as the key is found whereas failure requires a search through all the non-empty positions that are in the same equivalence class as the target. It follows that insertions will also take longer than successful searches. The technique of ordered hashing can be used to reduce the number of probes for unsuccessful searches (but not insertions).

The method utilises the simple idea that if the keys had been inserted in the directory in descending order then the search could be terminated as soon as it discovered a 'less than' key. Of course, in practice, we need to be able to insert keys in arbitrary order, as they arrive 'on-line'. The retrieve and insert algorithm given below implements an ordered hash directory.

```
type sparse array keytype of infotype =
class
const n = {size of directory}
type entry = record
                  key : keytype
                  info : infotype
              end;
var directory : array [0 .. n − 1] of directory;
        {ordered hash directory}
        i, p : 0 .. n − 1;

.
.
.

begin
function entry retrieve (k : keytype) : infotype;
        var found : boolean;
                  unsuccessful : boolean;
        begin
        i := h(k); p := i; {initial probe at i}
        found := false; unsuccessful := false;
        repeat
                  if directory [p].key = k then found := true
                  else if directory [p].key < k or p = i then unsuccessful := true (i)
                  else p := p ⊖ inc(k);
        until found or unsuccessful;
        if found then retrieve := directory [p].info
                  else {unsuccessful = true}
                            retrieve := undefined;
        end;
function entry insert (var k : keytype, var e : infotype, var status : (ok, fail));
        var inserted : boolean;
        begin
        i := h(k); p := i;        {initial probe at i}
        inserted := false;
        repeat
                  if directory [p].key = k then begin {update existing entry}
                            inserted := true;
                            directory [p].key := e
                  end
```

```
              else if directory[p].key = empty
                  then begin
                      inserted := true;
                      directory[p].key := k;
                      directory[p].info := e;
                  end
              else if directory[p].key < k then begin
                  {place new entry in order}
                  directory[p].key ⇔ k;                    (ii)
                  directory[p].info ⇔ e;
                  end;
              p := p ⊖ inc(k)                               (iii)
              until inserted or p = i;
              if inserted then status := ok
                  else status := fail;
      end;
  begin
  for p := 0 to n − 1 do directory[p].key := empty;
  end; {of class}
```

Line (*i*): to reduce the number of tests it is assumed that ∀ k, $k \in$ keytype $k >$ empty. *Line* (*ii*): ⇔ denotes interchange, the current value of k and e are inserted in the correct position, but the new values will now have to be inserted.

During insertion, the parameter k takes on a decreasing series of values and the increments in line (iii) will vary.

This is a rather peculiar state of affairs in spite of the innocuous appearance of the insert function, so it is helpful to consider an example.

Suppose an 11-entry directory contains eight non-empty entries with key values

$$97, 93, 58, 53, 45, 41, 31, 26$$

and that the linear quotient method is used to locate entries: thus $h(53) = 9$ and $\text{inc}(53) = 4$. The entries will, if entered in descending order, be distributed as shown in figure 11.3.

The reader may verify that the retrieve algorithm will indeed locate each of these entries correctly. Now if we wish to insert an entry with key value 52 ($h(52) = 8$, $\text{inc}(52) = 4$) the insert algorithm first replaces directory[8] by 52 and sets k to 45 ($\text{inc}(45) = 4$); after examining directory[4] it sets directory[4] to 45 and k to 26 ($\text{inc}(26) = 2$) which after trying directory[2] it successfully locates it in directory[0]. The directory containing all nine keys is therefore as shown in figure 11.4.

The retrieve algorithm works properly iff for every key $k = $ directory[j].key we do not have $k >$ directory[j'].key for some j' which appears earlier than j in the path corresponding to k. Since the insertion algorithm never decreases the value of any position it preserves this condition.

		h(k)	inc(k)

directory	0			
	1	53	9	4
	2	41	8	3
	3	58	3	5
	4	26	4	2
	5	93	5	8
	6			
	7	31	9	2
	8	45	1	4
	9	97	9	8
	10			

Figure 11.3 Before insertion

directory	0	26
	1	53
	2	41
	3	58
	4	45
	5	93
	6	
	7	31
	8	52
	9	97
	10	

Figure 11.4 After insertion of entry with key value = 52

Ordered hashing reduces the length of unsuccessful searches to the length of successful searches without increasing the cost per insertion. Therefore it is attractive where unsuccessful searches are common. The method is never useful in typical compiler applications where unsuccessful searches are almost always followed by insertions.

11.5 CHAINED HASHING

An obvious and effective solution to the problem of collision handling is to link all entries with identical primary hash positions, $h(k)$ together as a linked list. The elements of this list may be in a separate 'overflow area' or in the main directory itself.

In the method of *overflow with chaining* (figure 11.5) both the directory and the nodes of the overflow area contain a link field. At the expense of the extra space required for the pointers, this method is very effective.

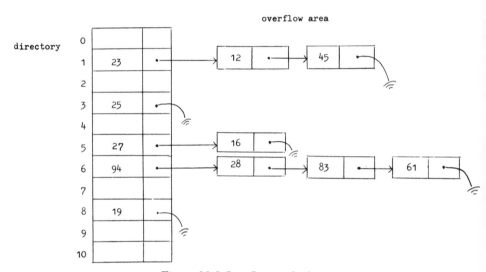

Figure 11.5 Overflow with chaining

A variation of this last technique is called *overflow with internal chaining* where the overflow entries are chained into the empty positions of the directory itself. Chaining in the overflows cannot be done until all the directory entries have been inserted since, until this moment, the unused entries are not known. Production of the final directory is, therefore, in two stages. Initially only non-overflow entries are stored in the directory. Once it is known that no new entries will be added, the overflow entries, which have been temporarily stored in an overflow area are chained into the empty positions. The redundant nodes in the overflow area may be returned to the reservoir. The main drawback of this method is that, since the complete structure of the directory cannot be determined until all the entries are known, it is not useful where new entries are constantly being added. The advantage is, of course, in the saving of space occupied in the overflow area.

The deletion of entries presents no great problem for either of the chaining methods, the unwanted entry is cleared to empty and if it is an overflow entry the node may be deleted from the chain and returned to the reservoir.

11.6 EFFICIENCY OF HASHING METHODS

The average search length for hashing methods depends very much on the load factor (percentage filled of the directory). The tables below give the average search lengths for the methods considered in this unit. In all cases it is assumed that there is a random distribution of keys.

	successful search						
% load factor	25	50	75	80	85	90	95
linear probing	1.167	1.500	2.500	3.000	3.833	5.500	10.500
quadratic search	1.163	1.443	2.011	2.209	2.472	2.853	3.521
linear quotient	1.151	1.386	1.848	2.012	2.232	2.558	3.153
overflow with chaining		1.250		1.400		1.450	1.500
overflow with internal chaining	1.137	1.305	1.518	1.570	1.611	1.676	1.738

	unsuccessful search						
% load factor	25	50	75	80	85	90	95
linear probing	1.389	2.500	8.500	13.000	22.720	50.500	200.500
quadratic search	1.371	2.193	4.636	5.810	7.715	11.400	22.040
linear quotient	1.333	2.000	4.000	5.000	6.667	10.000	20.000
overflow with chaining		1.107		1.249		1.307	1.300
overflow with internal chaining	1.037	1.180	1.495	1.589	1.694	1.812	1.946

How do hash methods compare with other search strategies (for example, binary search)? From the standpoint of speed they are better for large numbers of entries because the average search length stays bounded as the number of entries increases, if we ensure that the directory does not get too full.

It must be pointed out that hashing is inferior in other respects

(1) after an unsuccessful search we only know the key is not present, whereas binary searches give more information making it possible to find the largest key value less than k, etc.
(2) directory entries cannot (efficiently) be output in lexicographic order of key values
(3) hash methods are efficient only on *average*, while their worst case is terrible
(4) the deletion of entries for non-chained methods is extremely cumbersome.

To get full advantage from hashing as many as possible of the following criteria should be satisfied

(a) a fairly good approximate estimate of the number of entries should exist, and the directory should be made at least some 15 per cent larger
(b) the volume of data should not be highly variable
(c) the distribution of data should be random.

If none of these criteria is satisfied the alternative controlled scan strategies are to be preferred.

11.7 SUMMARY

1. Hashing techniques seek to place an entry at a position computed from its key. If that position is occupied, a collision occurs. The different techniques vary in how they handle the overflows resulting from collisions.

2. Hashing functions should be

(a)   distributed evenly across the set of directory positions

(b)   as random as possible

(c)   fast to evaluate.

3. Open hash methods locate overflows in the directory by using an increment function.

4. Ordered hash is an open hashing technique that reduces unsuccessful search time down to the time for successful searches.

5. Chained hash methods use linear linked list techniques to locate overflows.

6. Hashing is advantageous where the data are randomly distributed and non-variable. Average search lengths are a function of the directory load factor rather than directory size. The worst case search length for hashing can be very bad; hashing cannot easily provide other information about the contents of the directory.

11.8 BIBLIOGRAPHICAL NOTES

The most comprehensive account of hashing is contained in *The Art of Computer Programming*, vol. 3, *Sorting and Searching* (Knuth, 1973). The technique of ordered hashing is described in Amble and Knuth (1974).

12 *Recursion and Recursive Algorithms*

12.1 RECURSION

Before continuing with the treatment of search methods a full discussion of recursion is needed to prepare the ground for the next chapter on binary trees.

For the generation of programmers trained in the 1960s the word recursion had a special 'advanced' ring to it. To the practically minded Cobol or Fortran programmer it was a great time- and space-wasting irrelevance. To the curious it was mysterious and mystical. To the theoretical it was the acid-test of academic respectability. Recursion, and one's attitude to it was symptomatic of the great divide between academic and so-called commercial programming — Algol 60 on one hand and Cobol on the other. Hopefully the gap has been narrowed sufficiently for recursion to be seen in perspective. Unfortunately reputations are hard to live down and the purveyors of compilers still boast of 'advanced features' by which they mean recursion.

There is nothing intrinsically difficult about recursion. A *recursive* object is one that is defined partially in terms of itself. The idea of recursion occurs frequently in even elementary mathematics and therefore it should not surprise us that it is an important concept in programming. For example, the process of differentiating the product of two terms u, v is usually expressed by the rule

$$\frac{d}{dx}(uv) = u\frac{dv}{dx} + v\frac{du}{dx}$$

and it seems neither advanced or mysterious, to apply the same rule again if either u or v itself contains the product of two terms. What makes recursive algorithms appear difficult to those not familiar with them is a misguided attempt to understand them in terms of what the machine does, rather than in terms of what we are attempting to solve. The advantages of recursion are mainly conceptual, it fits naturally into our top-down, stepwise refinement approach to problem-solving. To differentiate a product, we break it into the simpler subproblems of differentiating the individual terms — if these terms themselves involve the product of terms, we deal with them by recursive application of the same rule. This aspect of recursion may be dubbed *divide and rule*, since the same procedure is applied to successively simpler subproblems until a case is found which is simple enough to be solved directly. For many

problems elegant solutions can be obtained by this approach. Consider the
problem of finding the maximum and minimum elements contained within a
consecutive section of an array s. Let l and u be the upper and lower limits of
the section. The obvious solution is

```
var s : array [1 .. m]of integer;
      l,u : 1 .. m;      {limits of section}
procedure minmax (var min, max : integer);
{minmax return the minimum and maximum values of the section
                                                    s[l] ... s[u]}

var i : integer;      {auxiliary ptr to scan section}
begin
min := s[l] ;
max := s[u] ;
i := l + 1;
while i ≤ u do begin
                 {compare max,min with rest of section}
                 if s[i] < min then min := s[i] ;
                 if s[i] > max then max := s[i] ;
                 i := i + 1
                 end;
     end;
```

An entirely different algorithm is suggested by the recursive divide and rule
approach.

(1) If s has length 2 or less then its maximum and minimum values can be
obtained directly.

(2) If s has length greater than 2 then its $\begin{Bmatrix} \text{maximum} \\ \text{minimum} \end{Bmatrix}$ value will be the
$\begin{Bmatrix} \text{maximum} \\ \text{minimum} \end{Bmatrix}$ of the two $\begin{Bmatrix} \text{maximum} \\ \text{minimum} \end{Bmatrix}$ values of the two subsections s_1, s_2

where

$$s_1 = s[l] \ldots s[(u + l) \text{ div } 2]$$
$$s_2 = s[u + l) \text{ div } 2 + 1] \ldots s[u]$$

(3) The maximum and minimum values of s_1, s_2 can be obtained by recursive
application of this procedure.

This leads to the following algorithm

```
procedure minmax(l, u : 1 .. m; var min, max : integer)
                 {l, u denote the limits of the section to be considered}
                 var h : 1 ... m;      {halfway point of section}
                 min1, max1, min2, max2 : integer;
```

```
                begin
                if u − l < 2 then begin
                                {section length ⩽ 2}
                                if s[l] < s[u] then begin
                                                        min := s[l]
                                                        max := s[u]
                                                    end
                                          else begin
                                                    min := s[u] ;
                                                    max := s[l]
                                                end
                else begin
                    h := (l + u) div 2;
                    minmax(l,h, min 1, max 1);
                    minmax(h + 1, u, min2, max2);
                    min := min (min1, min2);
                    max := max (max1, max2);
                end
        end;
```

This algorithm is altogether more transparent than the obvious solution and in this respect is to be preferred.

Another important aspect of recursion is the possibility of defining an infinite set of objects by a finite statement. Thus, syntactically, we may define the set of unsigned integers by the recursive BNF production

⟨unsigned integer⟩ ::= ⟨digit⟩ | ⟨digit⟩⟨unsigned integer⟩

In the same manner a recursive algorithm specifies an indefinite set of computations even when there are no explicit repetitions or iterations. But just as the BNF production specifies an infinite set of integers all of which are finite in length, a *well-formed* recursive algorithm defines an infinite set of computations all of which must terminate. However, because of the possibility of non-termination, it is incumbent on the programmer always to show that his algorithm terminates.

The necessary and sufficient language feature for expressing recursion is the procedure construct, which permits a group of statements to be referred to explicitly by names. Since recursive procedures are not circular they have a general form

```
    procedure P;
        begin
        if B then S
            else 𝒫
        end;
```

where B is a boolean escape condition, S is a sequence of statements not including a call of *P* and *𝒫* is a sequence of statements at least one of which includes a call on *P*. Proving that *P* terminates requires showing that *B* becomes true after a finite number of applications of *P*. Thus, in the minimax example, termination follows from the fact that $u - l \leqslant 2$ must become true after a finite number of halving operations, whatever the length of the initial section.

In general a procedure has associated with it a set of local objects which have no meaning outside the procedure body. This is the essence of the scope rules governing procedures. Each activation of recursive procedure necessarily requires a new set of local objects, the identifiers always referring to the most recently created set. The same rule applies to the parameters of procedures which by definition are bound to the procedure. The implementation of this mechanism implies that each activation of procedure has its own area of store for the current *activation record*, which can only be relinquished when the activation has terminated. As a consequence the depth of recursion involved in the execution of a recursive procedure governs the amount of store needed. It is therefore mandatory in all practical applications to show not only that the ultimate depth of recursion is finite, but that it is small enough to be accommodated in the available area of store. Where the storage overheads of a recursive algorithm are not suitably bounded then an iterative solution is imperative.

Generally speaking recursion should not be used where there is an equally good obvious iterative solution, but it should not be supposed from this that recursion is to be avoided at all costs. Where the underlying algorithm is naturally recursive then subject to its storage requirements, it should be used in the interests of clarity of program text. In some situations a compromise is possible whereby an iterative algorithm can be derived mechanically from the recursive one, the recursive algorithm can then serve as supporting documentation in the form of comment statements.

12.2 MECHANICS OF RECURSION

We must now discuss how recursive procedures may be implemented on what are, after all, essentially non-recursive computers. This is the basis of methods for eliminating recursion.

Each procedure call creates an activation record, consequently the implementation of recursion centres on the runtime handling of activation records. The significant property of recursive procedures is that any point in time the currently active call has to be completed before the immediately previous one can be resumed. In effect the calls, and with them their activation records, are organised on a last-in first-out (LIFO) basis. The number of such activation records is dependent on the depth of recursion. The natural structure for implementing recursion is therefore the sequence with the restriction that all accesses, additions and deletions occur at the same end. Such a structure is called a *stack*. The terminology of stacks owes much to the pushdown stacks of dinner

plates that are used in some self-service restaurants. We talk of *pushing* a new
activation record on to the *top* of the stack, and *popping* it off when the
activation has completed. The least accessible part of the stack is called the stack
bottom, and so on. Stacks not only provide an excellent mechanism for the
implementation of recursion but also for the implementation of all procedure
calls. On account of this many modern computers include special hardware
instructions for stack manipulation. The detailed structure of an activation
record depends on the particular procedure but in general it will contain space
for all objects local to the procedure, as well as the procedure parameters and
the program address of the statement to be obeyed after the call (the so-called
return address). Figure 12.1 represents a snapshot of the execution of the
recursive procedure *P* when the depth of recursion is 2.

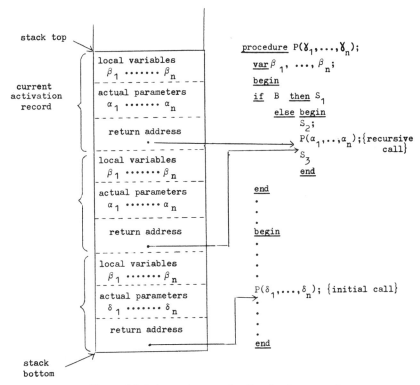

Figure 12.1 A runtime stack of activation records

A stack of activation records is more properly called an *information structure*
rather than a data structure, since its structure reflects the way in which
different instruction modules (that is, procedures) are connected dynamically
rather than the structure of the data.

Since stacks are a restricted form of sequence it goes without saying that any
implementation which supports efficient operations on one end of a sequence is

suitable for the implementation of stacks. Because of the availability of special hardware instructions, and because normally only one runtime stack is necessary, most language implementations use the contiguous array representation.

Many languages, such as Fortran, do not allow the recursive use of procedures; but this does not mean that naturally recursive operations cannot be programmed in these languages. The recursive structure of the algorithm has to be incorporated implicitly into the procedure itself; usually this is done by the explicit use of a stack. Because the recursion is not explicit, there is often no need for the activation records to contain explicit control information such as the return address. The transformation of recursive procedures into iterative ones is the subject of the next section.

12.3 REMOVAL OF RECURSION

The implementation of recursive procedures provides a general framework for the removal of recursion using stacks explicitly. Simplifications beyond this are possible for a number of classes of algorithm.

The simplest of all ways of eliminating recursion can be applied when the last action of procedure *P* is a recursive call of *P*. In this case simply replace the call of *P* by **goto** *P*.

For example, the linear search method on a linear linked list may be expressed recursively as

```
function isinlist (i : integer, l : list) : boolean;
       begin
       if l = nil then isinlist := false
       else
       if l ↑ .value = i then isinlist := true
              else isinlist := isinlist (i, l ↑ .link)
       end
```

Using the transformation rule this becomes

```
function isinlist (i : integer, l : list) : boolean;
       label start;
       begin
start : if l = nil then isinlist := false
       else
       if l ↑ .value = i then isinlist := true
                     else begin
                            l := l ↑ .link;
                            goto start
                            end
       end;
```

Which, bearing in mind the objections to the use of the **goto** statement for the purposes of iteration, can be rewritten in structured form as

```
function isinlist (i : integer, l : list) : boolean;
        var found : boolean;
        begin
        found := false;
        while not found and l ≠ nil
            do if l ↑ .value = i then found := true
                        else l := l ↑ .link;
        isinlist := found
        end
```

The familiar factorial function can be transformed using the same rule, though an extra variable is required to build up the result

```
function fac(n : integer) : integer : {n ⩾ 0}
        begin
        if n = 0 then fac := 1
                else fac := n * fac(n – 1)
        end;
```

becomes

```
function fac(n : integer) : integer;      {n ⩾ 0}
        label start;
        var f : integer;      {used to build result}
        begin
start : if n = 0 then f := 1
                else begin
                f := n * f;
                n := n – 1;
                goto start
                end;
        fac := f
        end
```

or in structured form

```
function fac(n : integer) : integer;    {n ⩾ 0}
        var f : integer;
        begin
        f := 1;
        while n ≠ 0 do begin
                        f := n * f;
                        n := n – 1
                        end;
        fac := f
        end;
```

This form of recursion, with only one recursive call, we shall refer to as *linear recursion.* Linear recursive procedures with the recursive call at the end of the procedure have such a simple and better iterative form that they seldom need to be used in their recursive form because their storage requirements are proportional to the depth of recursion reached, as opposed to a constant for their iterative form.

A more complex form of linear recursion occurs when the recursive call is not the final statement of procedure.

This more interesting class of linear recursive procedure includes the copy of a list procedure of section 8.5.

```
function copy (b : list) : list;
        {returns a pointer to a fresh copy of list b}
        begin
        if b = nil then
            else addfront(b ↑ .value, copy(b ↑ .link))
        end
```

The iterative version, which was also given in chapter 8, has two loops, the first of which uses the list r as a stack on to which the values of b are pushed. This leaves r containing the same value as list b, but in reverse order. The second loop pops the values off the stack and adds them on to the list a.

```
function copy(b : list) : list;
        {returns a pointer to a fresh copy of list b}
        var r : list;    {used as a stack}
            q : ↑ node;   {auxiliary ptr}
        begin
        q := b;
        a := nil;
        r := nil;
        while q ≠ nil do begin
            addfront(q ↑ .value, r);   {pushstack (q ↑ .value)}
            q := l ↑ .link
            end;
        while r ≠ nil do begin
            addfront(r ↑ .value, a);   {addfront(popstack, a)}
            r.deletefront;
            end;
        copy := a
        end;
```

It is now quite easy to see how the iterative version can be derived. In essence the recursive call is replaced by a **while** loop, but the values of $q.\uparrow$ value have to be saved on a stack to be available on 'return' from the call. The effect of stacking a series of values is to reverse their order so the second loop has to iterate in the reverse order from the first.

These considerations lead to a second rule: that linear recursive procedures of the general form

```
procedure f(x);
    begin
    if g(x) then h(x)
        else begin
            α;
            f(k(x));
            β
        end;
    end
```

can be rewritten in the form

```
procedure f(x);
    begin
    while not g(x) do begin
                α;
                x := k(x)
            end
    h(x);
    while x not back to its original value
                do begin
                    x := k⁻¹(x);
                    β
                end
    end
```

where $k^{-1}(x)$ is the inverse of the function $k(x)$ and none of the functions has side-effects on the parameter. If $k^{-1}(x)$ is not directly computable, then the sequence $x, k(x), k(k(x)), \ldots$, must be saved on a stack or in some other structure which may be accessed in reverse order. This rule, unlike the first, is not mechanical and may require some thought before it is applied.

Another useful linear recursive algorithm that falls into this class is the free format integer print routine.

```
procedure freeprint(i : integer);    {i ⩾ 0}
            var q : integer;    {quotient}
            begin
            if i < 10 then printdigit(i)
                else begin
                    q := i div 10;
                    freeprint(q);    {freeprint i without final digit}
                    printdigit(i − q * 10)    {print final digit}
                end
            end
```

It is left as an exercise for the reader to produce an iterative version of freeprint.

The removal of recursive calls from higher order recursive procedures is more complicated. The approach is to remove the calls one at a time using the rules for linear recursion. In general, however, the removal of recursion from higher order recursive procedures is often unprofitable because the iterative version will require a stack. Consequently there is usually only a slight gain in efficiency for a considerable loss of transparency.

12.4 RECURSION IN THE DESIGN OF ALGORITHMS

We now resume our discussion of the importance of recursion as a tool in problem-solving that can be used in conjunction with stepwise refinement. The idea is simple enough: we write down conditions which represent all cases in the problem. The simple ones we solve directly, the others by a recursive procedure. Depending on its complexity the resulting recursive procedure may be used as it stands or if desired in its iterative form. As an example consider the following simple problem (Griffiths, 1975).

A one-dimensional array of integers

a : **array** $[1 \ . . \ m]$ **of** integer

contains an ordered sequence of integers possibly with repetitions. It is required to find the integer which occurs most often in a. If the maximum is attained by more than one integer any solution may be given. The resulting value is called the 'mode' of the sequence. For example, in the sequence

$(1,1,3,3,3,3,6,7,7)$

the value of the mode is 3. (At this point the reader should try the problem.)

To adopt a recursive approach to finding the solution we must view a sequence of values

$a[1], a[2], \ldots, a[n]$

as a recursive structure

$$\text{sequence of length } n$$
$$\longleftarrow \quad \longrightarrow$$
$$a[1], a[2], \ldots, a[n-1], a[n]$$
$$\longleftarrow \quad \longrightarrow$$
$$\text{sequence of length } n-1$$

that is, sequence of length n = (sequence of length $n-1$).$a[n]$ for $n \geqslant 1$. The computation of the mode of a sequence of length n, requires two values regarding the sequence of length $n-1$

    value   = the mode of the sequence length $n - 1$
    number = the number of occurrences of the mode value

We are now in a position to enumerate all the cases concerning the mode of a sequence of length n.

Let mode(n) be a procedure returning result type

record
value : integer;   {mode value}
number : integer   {number of occurrences of mode value}
end

for a sequence of length n.

In all we can distinguish five cases

(1) $n = 1$

  mode(1).value = 1
  mode(1).number = $a[1]$

(2) $n > 1, a[n] \neq a[n-1]$

  This cannot cause a change of mode, therefore mode(n) = mode($n-1$).

(3) $n > 1, a[n] = a[n-1], a[n] = $ mode($n-1$).value

  This does not cause a change of mode, but it does increase the number of occurrences, therefore

  mode(n).number = mode($n-1$).number + 1

(4) $n > 1, a[n] = a[n-1], a[n] \neq$ mode $(n-1)$.value

  There are two possibilities depending on whether we have a long enough sequence of some values to change the mode. This can be determined by comparing $a[n - $ mode($n-1$).number$]$ with $a[n]$.

(a) if they are equal then we have a series of values that constitute a new mode

  mode(n).value = $a[n-1]$

and

  mode(n).number = mode($n-1$).number + 1

(b) if they are unequal then there is no change

  mode(n) = mode($n-1$)

for example, $a[7]$ will cause a change of mode

  iff $a[7] = a[7-3] = 5$
  $n = 1\ 2\ 3\ 4\ 5\ 6\ 7$
      $(1, 1, 1, 5, 5, 5, ?, \ldots)$
         ↑ ↑
         │ value 1
         │ number 3
       value 1
       number 3

After checking that we have covered all the possibilities, we must consider whether any simplification is possible by merging two or more of the cases. Looking at cases 3 and 4(a) we see that these both produce a change of mode, while cases 2 and 4(b) do not. This suggests that there may be some redundancy in the specification of the conditions. The crucial observation is that if $a[i]$ for some i, is a component of the sequence of values that form mode(n) then that sequence must start at element $a[i - \text{mode}(i - 1).\text{number}]$. This allows us to join conditions 3 with 4(a) and 2 with 4(b), reducing the cases to

(1) $n = 1$

      mode(1).value = $a[1]$
      mode(1).number = 1

(2) {cases 3 and 4(a)}

      $n > 1, a[n]_i = a[n - \text{mode}(n - 1).\text{number}]$

      that is, $a[n]$ is part of the mode(n) sequence

      mode(n).value = $a[n]$
      mode(n).number = mode($n - 1$).number + 1

(3) {cases 2 and 4(b)}

      $n > 1, a[n] \neq a[n - \text{mode}(n - 1).\text{number}]$

      that is, $a[n]$ is not part of the mode(n) sequence

      mode(n) = mode($n - 1$)

Using these three conditions we may construct a recursive algorithm

```
type modetype = record
                    value   : integer;
                    number : integer
                    end;
procedure mode(n : integer; var result : modetype);
            var p : modetype;   {result of mode(n − 1)}
            begin
            if n = 1 then with result
                    do begin    {case 1}
                        value := a[1] ;
                        number := 1
                        end
        else
        begin
        mode (n −1, p);   {evaluate mode(n − 1)}
        if a[n] = a[n − p.number]
            then begin   {case 2, a[n] part of mode sequence}
                with result do
```

```
                begin
                value := a[n] ;
                number := p.number + 1
                end

        end
    else    {case 3, a[n] not part of mode sequence}
        result := p;

end
end
```

This can be transformed into iterative form using the general rule for linear recursive procedures

```
procedure mode(n : integer; var result : modetype);
        var i : integer;
        begin
        with result do begin
                value := a[1] ;    {n = 1}
                number := 1;
                i := 1;
                while i ≠ n do
                        begin
                        i := i + 1;
                        if a[i] = a[i − number]
                            then begin
                                value := a[k] ;
                                number := number + 1
                                end;
                        end
                end
        end;
```

Experience suggests that this algorithm compares very favourably with the one likely to be obtained by intuition. By considering each case, first in isolation and then in relation to the others, we were able to spot the significance of the relation

$$a[i] = a[i − \text{number}]$$

which eliminates the redundant tests.

As with any systematic design method, we can informally verify the correctness of the solution because all working notes appear on paper and not solely as ephemeral thoughts. Of course these notes can also usefully serve as part of the final documentation.

We conclude this section with a further example, the derivation of a very good sort algorithm known as 'Quicksort' (Hoare, 1962).

The problem is to devise an algorithm to sort a sequence s of n elements, stored in an array

   a : **array** $[1 .. n]$ **of** integer

The divide and rule approach requires us to specify one or more simple cases which can be solved directly and a method of dealing recursively with all other situations. The simplest sequence to sort is one containing only one element. Our base condition is therefore 'To sort(s)

(1) If s has only one element then do nothing.'

It is tempting at this stage to crib directly from procedure minmax and postulate the recursive stage as

'(2) Partition s into two parts s_1, s_2; then sort(s_1), sort(s_2) by recursive application of this procedure.'

Unfortunately this is insufficient, since the instruction sequence sort(s_1), sort(s_2) does not correspond to sort(s); unless all the elements of s_1 are less than or equal to the elements of s_2. We must therefore reformulate the recursive stage as

'(2) Partition s into two parts s_1, s_2 such that all the elements of s_1 are less than or equal to the elements of s_2. Sort(s_1), sort(s_2) by recursive application of this procedure.'

Although this version is correct it turns out that it is easier to partition s into s_1, s_2, s_3, such that all elements of s_1 are less than or equal to s_2, all the elements of s_2 have the same value but in turn are less than or equal to s_3. This is also more efficient since there is no need to sort(s_2). In outline the quicksort algorithm becomes

```
procedure sort(s)
   begin
   if s contains more than one element
      then begin
            choose any element x from s;
            partition s into sequences
            s₁, s₂ and s₃ with elements
            less than or equal to, equal to,
            and greater than or equal to x, respectively;
            sort(s₁);
            sort(s₃)
            end
   end
```

Proceeding by stepwise refinement the next subproblem to be tackled is how to partition a sequence s. Partitioning a sequence $a[l] \ldots a[r]$ with respect to an

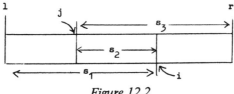

Figure 12.2

element x means, in effect, establishing three subsequences s_1, s_2, s_3, (figure 12.2) such that

$$s_1 : a[k] \leqslant x \text{ for all } k = 1 .. i - 1$$
$$s_3 : a[k] \geqslant x \text{ for all } k = j + 1 .. r$$

and

$$s_2 : a[k] = x \text{ for all } k = j + 1 .. i - 1$$

This can be produced iteratively by initially setting $i = 1$ and $j = r$ (figure 12.3) and moving i rightwards until an element $a_i > x$ is found, then moving j leftwards until an element $a_j < x$ is found. At this point we have established the

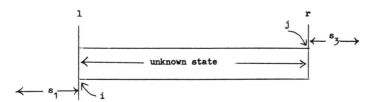

Figure 12.3

situation of figure 12.4, with a_i and a_j in the wrong partitions (unless $i > j$) so by interchanging a_i and a_j, we may continue expanding s_1 and s_2 by moving the pointers i and j. The process stops when i and j cross, that is, the area of unknown state has been reduced to zero.

The abstract definition of partitioning with respect to x is

$i := l; \ j := r;$
repeat
      while $a[i] < x$ **do** $i := i + 1$;   {expand s_1 until an element
                                                  probably in wrong partition}
      while $a[j] > x$ **do** $j := j - 1$;   {expands, until an element
                                                  probably in wrong partition}
      if $i \leqslant j$ **then begin**   {$a[i], a[j]$ definitely in wrong partitions}
                            $a[i] \Leftrightarrow a[j]$;   {interchange $a[i]$ and $a[j]$}
                            $i := i + 1$;
                            $j := j - 1$
                  end
  until $i > j$;

The most sensible choice of a value for x is the median element of the array.

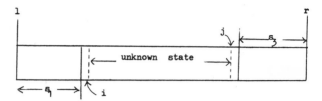

Figure 12.4

This is simple and efficient to find and will tend to split the sequences in half for each call on sort. The detailed version of quicksort therefore becomes

```
procedure sort (l, r : 1 .. n);
var i, j : 1 .. m; x : integer;   {l < r}
begin
if l < r then
       begin
       i := l; j := r;
       x := a[(l + r) div 2];   {partition wrt x}
       repeat
       while a[i] < x do i := i + 1;   {expand s₁}
       while a[i] > x do j := j − 1;   {expand s₃}
       if i ⩽ j then begin     {a[i], a[j] in wrong partitions}
                     a[i] ⇔ a[j];   {interchange}
                     i := i + 1;
                     j := j − 1
                     end
       until i > j;
       if l < j then sort(l,j);   {sort s₁}                    (i)
       if i < r then sort(i,r);   {sort s₃}                    (ii)
       end
end
```

Line (i), (ii): it saves an unnecessary call on sort to test whether s_1, or s_3 are empty before the call.

Quicksort is important as a sorting method because of its very fast expected runtime as compared to other methods. It does not perform so well, however, if the data are very nearly ordered in the first place.

12.5 CONCLUSION

Recursion, as a design method, is a useful tool which can be used in conjunction with stepwise refinement. By enumerating all the cases in a problem we can make our reasoning visible in the resulting program text. It is best used where the underlying problem or data are themselves inherently recursive or are capable of a simple recursive description.

At runtime recursion requires the overhead of a stack, which for many problems can be avoided by the use of iteration. In those cases where the interative version also requires a stack then explicit recursion is often preferable on the grounds of clarity. On modern computers, the trend towards hardware for handling stacks often invalidates the time inefficiency complaint against recursion.

Recursion is an essential item in the programmers' 'tool-kit' but it is one that needs to be justified before being used explicitly at runtime.

12.6 SUMMARY

1. A recursive object is one that is defined partially in terms of itself.
2. Recursion is primarily a problem-solving, 'divide and conquer' tool
(a) consider all the cases in a problem or situation
(b) solve the simple cases directly
(c) solve the other cases by recursive application of the procedure
(d) check the conditions for redundancies and omissions; if any are found, correct and recheck the solution.
3. Recursive procedures are often transparent and short.
4. Practical use of recursive procedures requires justifying that
(a) the ultimate depth of recursion is finite and that the stack can be accommodated in the available store
(b) the iterative equivalent algorithm is in some sense inferior.
5. Recursive procedures can always be made iterative by the explicit use of a stack.

12.7 BIBLIOGRAPHICAL NOTES

The treatment of recursion is based on the approach of 'Structured Programming with Gotos' (Knuth, 1974) and chapter 2 of *Algorithms + Data Structures = Programs* (Wirth, 1975). The rule for the elimination of general linear recursive calls and the mode exercise are due to Griffiths (1975).

13 *Binary Search Trees*

13.1 INTRODUCTION

Chapter 10 on search methods postponed discussion of binary search directories which may vary dynamically. We shall now remedy that omission. To calculate the average search length of a binary search the set of possible paths through the directory was represented by a binary tree (figure 13.1).

Binary trees thereby suggest themselves as a natural abstraction for binary search directories. Binary trees are clearly recursive and hence dynamic because each node of the binary tree has two subtrees which are themselves binary trees. The base case of the recursion is that binary trees may also be empty. A closer look at figure 13.1 reveals that for each node in the binary tree form of the directory the following condition is true: all nodes in its left subtree contain a value less than its value whereas those in the right subtree have a value greater than its value.

This is a condition applicable to binary search directories that does not (necessarily) apply to binary trees arising from other contexts.

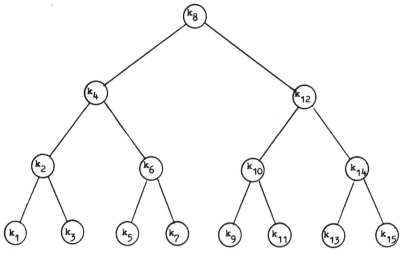

Figure 13.1 Binary tree form of ordered directory $(k_1, k_2, \ldots, k_{15})$

(i)   **graph**

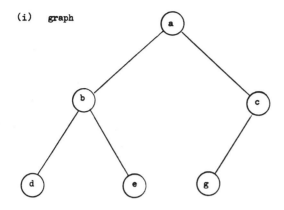

(ii) parenthesised form - (left, value, right)

((d, b, e), a, (g, c, ( )))

(iii) nested

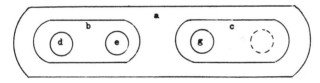

(iv) indentation - value, left, right

```
a
    b
        d
        e
    c
        g
        ( )
```

(v) parenthesised form - (value, left, right)

(a, (b, d, e), (c, g, ( )))

Figure 13.2 Some diagrammatic and textual representations of binary trees

Informally we define a **binarytree** structure to be either (1) empty or (2) a node comprising

(a)   a *left* subtree which is a binary tree
(b)   a *value* field which contains an item
(c)   a *right* subtree which is a binary tree.

We have the picture of a binary tree as a skeletal structure of nodes with each node containing an item. Although there is a distinction between a node and the

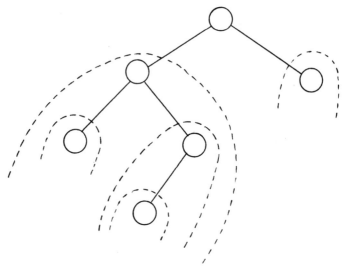

Figure 13.3 Nested hierarchy of binary trees

(i)   1976 FA Cup Winners =

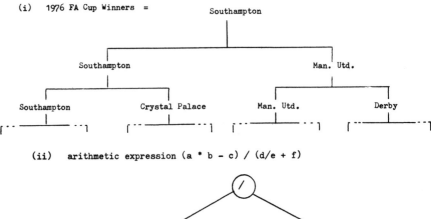

(ii)   arithmetic expression (a * b - c) / (d/e + f)

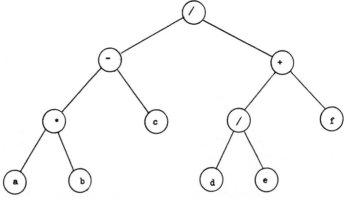

Figure 13.4 Some other uses of binary trees

item it contains, in keeping with standard practice we often do not make it where there can be no confusion.

Binary trees have several diagrammatic and textual representations. For example, if the items are of type letter then the same abstract binary tree can be presented in a number of different ways. (See figure 13.2.)

The most usual diagrammatic representation is the graph form, which clearly brings out the hierarchical relationship between nodes. Unlike natural trees binary trees are conventionally drawn with their root uppermost, and grow downwards (figure 13.3).

Binary trees can occur in other contexts apart from binary searching, for example, as the record of a sports knockout competition or as the structure of an arithmetic expression (figure 13.4).

The terminology for binary trees, although extensive, is intuitively clear. Each non-empty binary tree, t, has a *root* node which, in the graph form, is the node without any branches entering it from any other node in t. Thus in figure 13.2, the root is the node with item value a. The root node of the left (right) subtree of a binary tree, t, is called the left (right) *son* of the root of t, and the root of t is the *father* of its sons.

There are many obvious extensions, for example, in figure 13.5, the nodes containing t_2 and t_3 are said to be *brothers*, t_4, t_5 and t_6 are *grandsons* of t_1. Similarly the terms *ancestor* and *descendant* are used to denote relationships

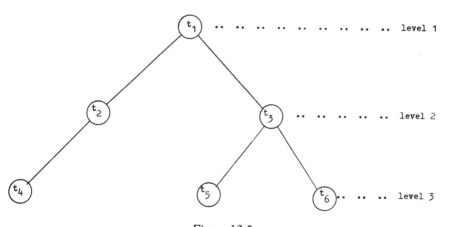

Figure 13.5

covering several levels of binary tree t. (The *level* of a node t_i with respect to the root of a binary tree, t, is defined by the recursive rule that the root of t has level 1, and the level of t_i is one greater than its father.) The terms t_4, t_5, and t_6 are said to be stored at *leaf* or *terminal* nodes of the binary tree. Terminal nodes and nodes with one son missing (for example, t_2) are also known as *final* nodes of t.

13.2 OPERATIONS ON BINARY TREES

We shall denote the general form of a binary tree type by

type T = **binarytree of** itemtype

which by analogy with sequence types can be considered to be shorthand for the schema

rectype T = **record**
                case tag   : (empty, nonempty) **of**
                empty   : ();
                nonempty : **record**   {type node}
                                left : T;   {left subtree}
                                value : itemtype;   {item}
                                right : T {right subtree}
                                end;
        end :

    The distinction between sequences and binary trees is that whereas the sequence schema is linearly recursive the schema for binary trees is doubly recursive.

    To discuss operations on binary trees without specifying their implementation in advance we need a set of abstract operations on binary trees. The basic operations are those that allow the accessing and updating of the tag and the component fields of a binary tree.

    t.tag
    t.left   the tag and component
    t.value   fields of a binary tree t
    t.right

We specify the initialisation of t as an empty binary tree by t.init.
    All assignments of binary trees must be implemented using a copy operation which we denote by

    t_1.assign (t_2) – makes a copy of t_2 and assigns it as the value of t_1

    To perform the selective updating of binary trees we need pointers into the subtrees of a binary tree. For this purpose we use pointers to binary trees

    p : ↑ **binarytree of** itemtype

    These can be dynamically bound to a particular instance of a binary tree by use of the 'address of' operator, @, where

    p := @(t)

sets p pointing to the root of the tree t. The components of the tree 'where p

points' may be accessed in the normal manner for pointers. Thus the instruction sequence

$p := @(t)$;
print($p \uparrow$ .left.value)

where t has the value shown in figure 13.6, would cause the value 7 to be printed.

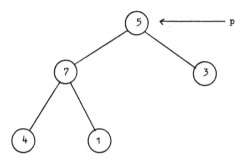

Figure 13.6 The tree t

These operations allow us to write algorithms for simple operations such as finding the leftmost final node of a tree.

```
var t : binarytree of integer;
    p : ↑ binarytree of integer;   {p points to t}
begin
if t.tag = empty then print ("t is empty")
    else begin
        p := @t;   {set p to point to t}
        while p ↑ .left.tag ≠ empty
            do p := @(p ↑ .left);
        print (p ↑ .value)
        end;
end
```

The controlled updating of binary trees requires their growth and contraction by a single item at a time. If t is an empty binary tree then the assignment

t.assign(( ), v, ( ))

adds a single terminal node, value v, to t. Because it is used so frequently we abbreviate this to

t.assignitem (v)

New nodes can be added to non-empty binary trees by use of a pointer to an empty subtree. Thus the algorithm

$p := @(t)$;
while $p \uparrow$ .left.tag $\neq$ empty
    do $p := @(p \uparrow$ .left);
$p \uparrow$ .left.assignitem(v)

extends the binary tree by an extra node, with value v, as its leftmost son.

The contraction of a binary tree by one node can be achieved by the assignment of an empty binary tree to a sub binary tree consisting of a single terminal node. This operation is denoted by

t.delete   {t must initially contain a single node}

which corresponds to the assignment

t.assign(())

Thus we may delete the leftmost terminal node of a binary tree t by

$p := @(t)$
while $p \uparrow$ .left.tag $\neq$ empty **or** $p \uparrow$ .right.tag $\neq$ empty **do**
    begin
    while $p \uparrow$ .left.tag $\neq$ empty
        do $p := @(p \uparrow$ .left);
    if $p \uparrow$ .right.tag $\neq$ empty
        then $p := @(p \uparrow$ .right);
    end;
{$p \uparrow$ .left.tag = empty **and** $p \uparrow$ .right.tag = empty}
$p \uparrow$ .delete

If it is required to delete the root of a non-empty subtree then the binary tree node values must be rearranged so that the deletion may be performed at a terminal node.

The addition and deletion of items from binary trees is more complex than for sequences because binary trees have a variable number of 'ends' where the updating may take place.

13.3 BINARY SEARCH TREES

Binary search directories can be conveniently represented by a binary tree of entries which conforms to the following conditions: the left subtree of a node contains only entries with keys less than the key of the node, while the right subtree contains only entries with keys greater than it. This condition (and, of course, its mirror image) is known as the *binary search invariant* for binary trees. It must be true before all directory operations if they are to work correctly, and consequently each operation must also leave it true.

As an example of a binary search tree consider a directory of 15 entries and

type keytype = **array** [1 . . 3] **of** letter

(see figure 13.7).

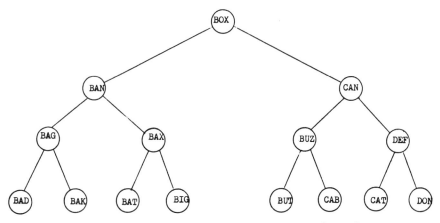

Figure 13.7 A binary tree satisfying the binary search requirement

The abstract form of a binary search may be specified as

```
begin
searcharea ← directory;     {set searcharea to cover the whole directory}
found := false;
while not found and not searcharea.empty
        do if searcharea.middle < target
                then searcharea.rightpart
                else if searcharea.middle > target
                        then searcharea.leftpart
                else found := true;
{either found := true and searcharea.middle = target
        or found := false and target is not in directory}
end
```

This algorithm can be rewritten directly in terms of binary tree operations to provide a locate function for use in a class implementing a sparse mapping.

```
type sparse array keytype of infotype =
class
type entry = record
                key : keytype;
                info : infotype
                end;
```

```
    var directory : binarytree of entry;    {obeys binary search invariant}
              p : ↑ binarytree of entry;    {ptr to searcharea subtree}
    entry size : integer;
        found : boolean;
begin
procedure locate (k : keytype);
        begin
        p := @(directory);    {set p to cover whole directory}
        found := false;
        while not found and p ↑ .tag ≠ empty
            do if p ↑ .value.key < k
                      then p := @(p ↑ .right)
                  else if p ↑ .value.key > k
                          then p := @(p ↑ .left)
                      else found := true;
        end;

function entry retrieve (k : keytype) : infotype
        begin
        locate(k);
        if found then retrieve := p ↑ .value.info
        else retrieve := undefined
        end;

procedure entry insert (k : keytype, i : infotype);
    •
    •
    •

procedure entry remove (k : keytype);
    •
    •
    •

begin
            directory.init;
            size := 0
end;
```

Because binary trees are recursive structures we should not be surprised that there is also a simple recursive version of locate. It can be derived in the normal manner by considering all the relationships that may exist between the key of the value of a binary tree and the target

```
procedure locate (k : keytype);    {recursive version}
        procedure loc (k : keytype; q : ↑ binarytree of entry);
        begin
        if q ↑ .tag = empty then found := false
        else if q ↑ .value.key < k then loc(k, @(q ↑ .right))
```

```
else if q ↑ .value.key > k then loc(k, @(q ↑ .left))
else begin
      found := true;
      p        := q
      end;
   end;
   begin
   loc(k, @(directory))                                          (i)
   end
```

Line (i): this call sets in motion the recursive calls.

The recursive locate would seem to have little to offer in the way of extra transparency and is less efficient storewise than the iterative version. However, as we shall see, recursion does have advantages when we consider the insertion and deletion of entries from binary search directories.

A binary search directory can be constructed by inserting each new entry as a new node at a bottom level of the binary tree. To maintain the binary search invariant the correct father must, of course, be located prior to the addition. For example, a new entry with key BAR can only be added to the directory shown in figure 13.7 as the left son of BAT.

The recursive version of the class procedure insert is straightforward

```
procedure entry insert (k : keytype; i : infotype);
      var newentry : entry;
      procedure ins (this : entry; p : ↑ binarytree of entry);
            begin
            if
            p ↑ .value.key < this.key then
                  if p ↑ .right.tag ≠ empty then ins(this, @(p ↑ .right))
                        else begin
                              p ↑ .right.assignitem(this);
                              size := size + 1
                              end
            else if
            p ↑ .value.key > this.key then
                  if p ↑ .left.tag ≠ empty then ins(this @(p ↑ .left))
                        else begin
                              p ↑ .left.assignitem(this);
                              size := size + 1
                              end

            {else do nothing, directory contains entry with key = k at p ↑}
            end;
      begin    {body of procedure insert}
      newentry := (k, i);
```

```
              if directory.tag = empty then begin
                                          directory.assignitem(this);
                                          size := 1
                                          end
              else ins(newentry, @(directory));
              end
```

The pointer p is moved down the directory, according to the binary search invariant, until a final mode is found, then the addition is made.

This algorithm may be transformed into an iterative version using the methods of the last chapter. A simplification can be made by replacing the forward testing for a final node by the introduction of an extra pointer t to remember the father of p.

```
     procedure entry insert (k : keytype; i : infotype);
          var this : entry
                    p, t : ↑ binarytree of entry;    {t ↑ is the father of p ↑}
                    found : boolean;
          begin
          newentry := (k, i);
          if directory.tag = empty then begin
                                      directory.assignitem(this);
                                      size := 1
                                      end
          else begin
              p := @(directory);
              found := false;
              while not found and p ↑ .tag ≠ empty
                        do begin
                            t := p;    {t remembers p}
                            if p ↑ .value.key < k then p := @(p ↑ .right)
                            else
                            if p ↑ .value.key > k then p := @(p ↑ .left)
                            else
                            found := true
                            end;
              if not found then    {make addition}
                        begin
                        if t ↑ .value.key > k then
                                    t ↑ .left.assignitem(this)
                        else t ↑ .right.assignitem(this);
                        size := size + 1
                        end;
              end
     end;
```

On average the depth of the recursion is proportional to $\log_2 n$ where n is the number of nodes in the binary tree. The iterative algorithm is thus marginally more efficient storewise but is less transparent than the recursive version.

There are two distinct cases to be dealt with when considering the removal of directory entries.

(1)   Entries stored at terminal nodes can be removed directly by the deletion of the node.
(2)   Entries stored at nodes with one or two non-empty subtrees have to be removed by a two-stage process.
    (a)   Find a replacement entry from a lower level of the directory. The replacement entry is used to overwrite the entry to be removed, and hence it must preserve the binary search invariant, that is, it must be the directory entry with key value next largest or smallest to the entry to be removed.
    (b)   The replacement entry can then be removed, from its original position in the directory, by recursive application of this procedure.

For the directory shown in figure 13.8, the entry with key BAT can be deleted directly. But the entry with key BUS can only be removed by finding a replacement for it, that is BOY or BXY. Since these are not at terminal nodes a replacement is needed, BYE in the case of BXY or BOU for BOY. No further recursive calls are necessary since both BYE and BOU are at terminal nodes and

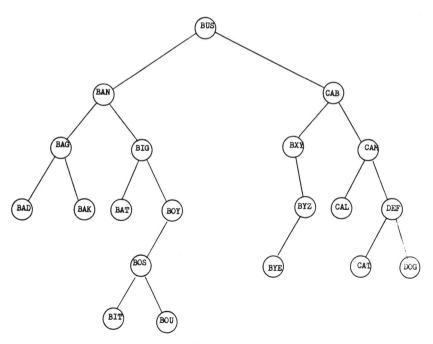

Figure 13.8

can be deleted directly. The resulting directory after the sequence
BUS ← BXY ← BYE is shown in figure 13.9.

The operation remove, in the context of the sparse mapping class, requires a single parameter, the key of the entry to be deleted. The procedure locate can be used to search for the node with the entry to be deleted. The class procedure remove can be written as

```
procedure entry remove (k : keytype);
    function replacement (q : ↑ binarytype of entry) : ↑ binarytree of entry;
            begin    {finds a replacement for q ↑ .value}
            if q ↑ .left ≠ empty
            then begin    {find rightmost left descendant}
                q := @(q ↑ .left);
                while q ↑ .right.tag ≠ empty do q := @(q ↑ .right);
                end
            else    {p ↑ .right.tag = empty}
                begin    {find leftmost right descendant}
                q := @(q ↑ .right);
                while q ↑ .left.tag ≠ empty do q := @(q ↑ .left);
                end;
            replacement := q;
            end;
    procedure removeit(p : ↑ binarytree of entry);
            var t : ↑ binarytree of entry;
            begin
            if p ↑ .left.tag = empty and p ↑ .right.tag = empty
                    then p↑ .delete    {delete node}
                    else begin
                        t := replacement(p);
                        p ↑ .value := t ↑ .value;                    (i)
                        removeit(t)
                        end;

            end;
    begin    {body of remove}
    locate (k);
    if found then begin
                removeit(p);
                size := size − 1;

                end
    end;
```

The procedure removeit can be made iterative very simply, since the only recursive call occurs at the end of the procedure body.

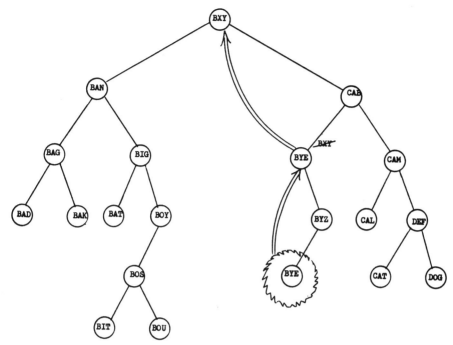

Figure 13.9 The directory after deleting the entry with key BUS using the sequence BUS ← BXY ← BYE

13.4 THE SHAPE OF BINARY SEARCH TREES

At any particular point in time the shape of a binary search tree will depend on the dynamic order of the insertions and removes that created directory. For example, consider the simple case of a set of entries with key values {BUS, BAN, CAB, BAG, BIG, BXY, CAM}. If the entries are inserted in that order then the resulting directory has the shape shown in figure 13.10.

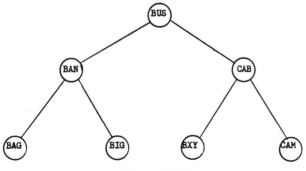

Figure 13.10

This binary search tree has the optimal average search length of

$$\frac{1 + 2 \times 2 + 4 \times 3}{7} \approx 2.43$$

If the entries had been inserted in the order {BAN, BAG, BIG, BXY, BUS, CAM, CAB} a less efficient binary search results (figure 13.11).

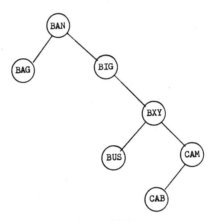

Figure 13.11

The average search length for this tree is

$$\frac{1 + 2 \times 2 + 1 \times 3 + 2 \times 4 + 1 \times 5}{7} = 3$$

The worst case is when the keys are inserted in order (or reverse order); the binary search tree degenerates into a sequence and with it the binary search into a linear search with average search length 4. (See figure 13.12.)

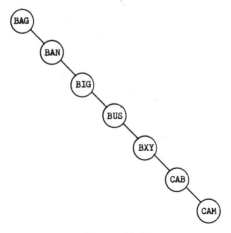

Figure 13.12

The shape of the binary search tree clearly determines the efficiency of the binary search algorithm. The optimal binary tree for a given set of entries has minimal height and is well balanced in the sense that the root of every subtree of the binary tree has as many left descendants as it has right descendants. Such binary search trees have the same average search length as a binary search on an ordered array, that is, $\sim\log_2 n$. In practice when there are dynamic insertions and deletions we are unlikely to maintain a perfectly balanced search tree. The question is just how bad is a 'random' binary search. More precisely we should like to know the average of search length averaged over all $n!$ binary search trees which can be obtained from the $n!$ distinct orderings of the keys. An analysis reveals that for large n the ratio is

$$\frac{\text{A random}}{\text{A balanced}} = 2 \log 2 \approx 1.386$$

in other words, given that all the keys are accessed with equal probability, the average 'random' binary search tree is only 39 per cent worse than the perfectly balanced case. Of course the *worst* random binary search tree, although unlikely to occur if all the orderings of the n keys are equally likely, is much worse than this.

The development of insert and remove algorithms that maintain well-balanced binary search trees lies outside the scope of this book. But it is worth noting that the figure of 39 per cent imposes a limit on the amount of extra work that may profitably be spent reorganising the binary search tree structure on insertion or removal of entries.

13.5 IMPLEMENTATION OF BINARY TREES

We introduced binary trees to serve as an abstract model for dynamic binary search directories. Because binary trees have essentially a dynamic nature they should therefore normally only be used to model dynamic structures. 'Static binary trees' are better considered to be array structures.

The principal implementation scheme for binary trees is dynamic and is a generalisation of linear linked lists. Each non-empty binary subtree is represented by a two-pointer node

```
type node = record
            left : ↑node;
            value : itemtype;
            right : ↑node
            end
```

(figure 13.13) in which each subtree is represented by a ↑node value. A complete binary tree is represented by a single ↑node value to the root node.

```
type binarytree of item = ↑node
```

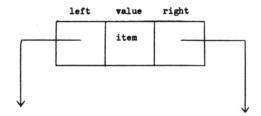

Figure 13.13

Thus the binary tree *t* in figure 13.14 is represented by figure 13.15.
    Storage management for linked binary trees can be handled by the same
reservoir structure that is used for linear linked structures. Thus we may

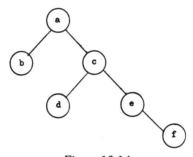

Figure 13.14

implement the assignment of binary trees by a simple recursive copy function
that uses a reservoir free.

```
function copy(t : ↑ node) : ↑ node;
        {copies the entire binary tree t, and returns a pointer to the root
        node}
        var r : ↑ node;
        begin
        if t = nil then copy ≔ nil
            else begin
                r ≔ free.acquire;
                r ↑ .left ≔ copy(t ↑ .left);
                r ↑ .right ≔ copy(t ↑ .right);
                r ↑ .value ≔ t ↑ .value;
                copy ≔ r
                end
        end
```

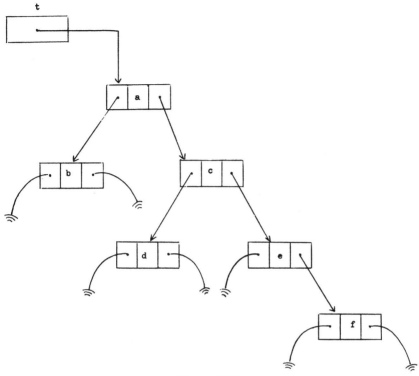

Figure 13.15

Because of the importance of the two-pointer methods we give the complete sparse mapping class using this implementation.

```
type sparse array keytype of infotype =
class    {uses reservoir free}
type entry = record
                key : keytype;
                info : infotype
                end;
        node = record
                left : ↑ node;
                value : ↑ entry;
                right : ↑ node
                end;
        binarytree = ↑ node;
var directory : binarytree;
            p : ↑ node;
        found : boolean;
    entry size : integer;
```

```
begin
procedure locate(k : keytype);
      begin
      p := directory;   {set p to cover whole directory}
      found := false;
      while not found and p ≠ nil
            do if p ↑ .value.key < k
                        then p := p ↑ .right
                  else if p ↑ .value.key > k
                              then p := p ↑ .left
                  else found := true
      end;
function entry retrieve(k : keytype) : infotype;
      locate(k);
      if found then retrieve := p ↑ .value.info
                  else retrieve := undefined
      end;


procedure insert(k : keytype; i : infotype);
      var newentry : entry;
      t : ↑ node;
      procedure ins(this : entry; p : ↑ node);
            begin
            if
            p ↑ .value.key < this.key then
                  if p ↑ .right ≠ nil then ins(this, p ↑ .right)
                  else begin     {new right son}
                        t := free.acquire;
                        t ↑ .value := this;
                        t ↑ .left := nil; t ↑ .right := nil;
                        p ↑ .right := t;
                        size := size + 1
                        end

            else if
            p ↑ .value.key > this.key then
                  if p ↑ .right ≠ nil then ins(this, p ↑ .right)
                        else begin     {new left son}
                              t := free.acquire;
                              t ↑ .value := this;
                              t ↑ .left := nil; t ↑ .right := nil;
                              p ↑ .left := t;
                              size := size + 1
                              end
                  {else do nothing, directory contains an entry with key = k}
                  end;
```

```
                begin
                newentry := (k, i);
                if directory = nil then begin
                                        directory := free.acquire;
                                        directory ↑ .left := nil;
                                        directory ↑ .right := nil;
                                        directory ↑ .value := this;
                                        size := 1
                                        end
                else ins(this, directory)
                end;
procedure entry remove(k : keytype);
    function replacement(q : ↑ node) : ↑ node;
            begin
            if q ↑ .left ≠ nil
                then begin
                        q := q ↑ .left;
                        while q ↑ .right ≠ nil do q := q ↑ .right;
                        end;
                else   {q ↑ .right ≠ nil}
                            begin
                            q := q ↑ .right;
                            while q ↑ .left ≠ nil do q := q ↑ .left
                            end;
                replacement := q;
            end;
procedure removeit (var p : ↑ node);                                    (i)
        var t : ↑ node;
        begin
        if p ↑ .left = nil and p ↑ .right = nil
                    then begin
                            free.return(p);
                            p := nil;
                            end
                    else begin
                            t := replacement(q);
                            p ↑ .value := t ↑ .value;
                            removeit(t)
                            end
        end;
        begin
        locate(k);
        if found then begin
                    removeit(p);
                    size := size − 1
                    end;
```

```
        end
begin
        directory := nil;
            size := 0;
    end;
```

Line (i): the procedure removeit requires *p* to be a **var** parameter, since the value nil is to be assigned to the link in the binary tree which previously contained *p* ↑. This would not be necessary if the method of making an empty tree involved only making an assignment to *p* ↑ (for example, *p* ↑ .value.tag := empty) rather than to the link that contains *p*.

There is a number of semi-linked methods of representing binary trees in which the storage of two nodes in consecutive store locations can indicate that the second is the left son of the first. Each non-empty subtree is a node

```
type node = record
                value : itemtype;
                right : ↑ node;
                left : boolean    {true iff neighbour is left son}
            end
```

The nodes of the binarytree have to be stored in a specific order known as *preorder*

(1)   first the root node
(2)   the nodes of the left subtree
(3)   the nodes of the right subtree.

The binary subtree *t* shown in figure 13.14 is stored as shown in figure 13.16.

Since only a single bit is required for the left tag field this method leads to a saving in store occupancy especially on machines with a small word length where a tag and pointer may fit in one word but two pointers will not. Although not as

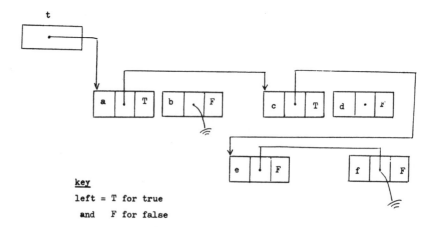

key
left = T for true
and   F for false

Figure 13.16

flexible as the two-pointer method, some freedom persists from not having to store distinct subtrees contiguously.

A variation on this method is to have two node variants each of which can be tightly packed in an integral number of words.

```
type node = record
            case tag : (rightsub, leftsub) of
            rightsub : ↑ node;
            leftsub : record
                      value : itemtype;
                      left : boolean    {true iff neighbour is left son}
                      end
            end
```

Essentially nil right pointers are omitted, those nodes with non-empty right subtrees are preceded by a rightsub variant node. For example the binary tree *t* in figure 13.14 is stored as shown in figure 13.17.

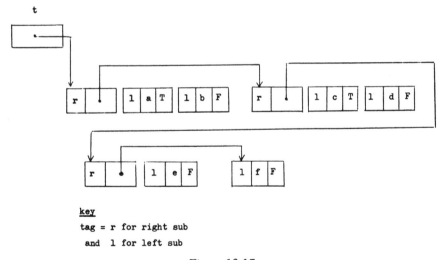

key
tag = r for right sub
and l for left sub

Figure 13.17

There is a number of completely contiguous schemes for implementing binary trees; the one-dimensional representations of binary trees can be easily adopted as storage structures. All that is required is a suitable internal representation of the punctuation characters. For example, the one-dimensional preorder representation of the binary tree *t* used above is

$(a, b, (c, d(e, , f)))$

The contiguous implementations are especially useful when inputting or outputting binary trees or moving them to backing store. A disadvantage of all pointer methods, of course, is that the pointers have no direct external representation, and hence make the binary trees non-relocatable in main store.

13.6 CONCLUSION

In this chapter we have considered the use of binary trees for the implementation of sparse mappings. In this context they have a number of advantages when the directory structure is highly variable, because not only do they have very reasonable search times but they also provide for simple implementations of other functions to do with ordering. Thus we may easily find the largest or smallest keys in the directory, and so on. However, it should not be supposed that binary searching is the only use of binary trees. Many relationships are hierarchical and can be conveniently represented by trees, and all trees have corresponding binary trees (see exercise 3.11) which can be used for the purposes of representation.

13.7 SUMMARY

1. A binary tree is either
(a) empty or
(b) a node comprising (i) a left subtree of type binary tree, (ii) a value field containing an item, (iii) a right subtree of type binary tree.
2. Insertion and deletion of nodes can only be performed at the final nodes of a binary tree.
3. Binary search trees are binary trees which satisfy the following invariant condition: for each node, the left(right) subtree of the node contains only entries with keys less than the key of the node, while the right(left) subtree contains only entries greater than it.
4. The shape of the binary search tree determines the efficiency of the search. On average, random binary trees are only 39 per cent worse than perfectly balanced binary trees.

13.8 BIBLIOGRAPHICAL NOTES

Binary trees and binary search trees are fundamental topics in computer science. Knuth (1968 and 1973) and Wirth (1975) contain a fuller account of the material in this chapter. The concept of balanced binary search trees is due to Adelson-Velskii and Landis (1962).

Exercises 3

3.1 Consider the procedure remove, in section 13.5, for a *linked binary search tree*. It can be optimised by taking as a separate case the removal of an entry stored at a node with only one binary subtree. Design such an algorithm.

3.2 An alternative method for the removal of entries from a *linked binary search tree* is: replace the node to be removed by its right binary subtree, and put its left binary subtree as the left binary subtree of its successor node (that is, the leftmost node of its binary subtree).

Using this method, removing the entry with key BAN from the figure

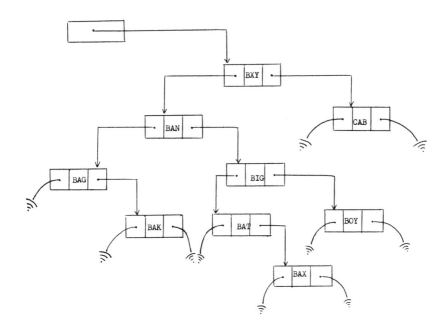

results in :

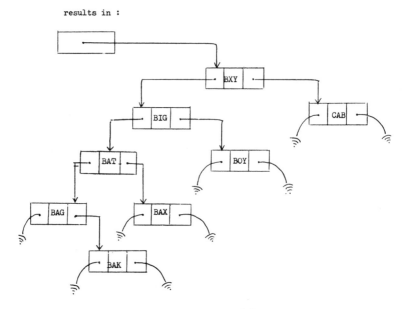

Figure Exercise 3.2

(a)   write an algorithm based on this method
(b)   contrast this method in respect of its effect on binary tree balance with
       the one given in chapter 13, and with the modified version of exercise 3.1.

3.3 A large directory is to be represented in the main store of a computer. To
achieve fast search times a hashing method is to be used. However, it is necessary
to be able to print the directory entries in order of the keys, and for this purpose
the entries are to be linked as a binary search tree. Design a class for this
structure with the operations

(a)   locate (k : keytype)
(b)   insert (k : keytype; i : infotype)
(c)   printinorder.

3.4 An application program processes several variables of type (sparse) **set of**
integer (cardinality in range $0 \dots 10^3$); an analysis of the program reveals that
the following operations (in order of relative frequency of usage) are required

(1) s.ascending(f)	which is to apply some procedure f to all the elements of
$\quad$ s.descending(f)	a set s in either ascending or descending order. (Note:
	the body of procedure f may be assumed as given, and
	therefore f need only be called when required.)
(2) s.has(i)	boolean function, returns true iff i is a member of s.
(3) s.insert(i)	a procedure that updates s by inserting integer i.

(4)*s*.empty   boolean function, returns true iff the set *s* is empty.

(5)*s*.remove(*i*)   a procedure that updates *s* by removing integer *i*.

(a) Devise a suitable storage structure for the type **set of** integer. State explicitly any invariant relation that it satisfies.

(b) Outline algorithms for each of the above operations and where possible give estimates of their computational cost. Make clear any assumptions on which your estimates are based.

3.5 Describe searching methods for dealing with collisions in open hash tables. Which of these methods is more suitable for (a) a Digital Equipment Corporation PDP-8 (b) an ICL 1906S? How can these methods be modified to deal with deletions from the table?

Use the linear quotient method to construct a table for the following set of keys

$$11, 4, 25, 12, 9, 28, 30$$

and for each entry give the number of probes required.

3.6 In a filing system the catalogue of all the files is organised as a binary search tree. Each entry contains a file name and, among other things, the date of its last access, encoded as an integer. Design a procedure to delete all the files in the catalogue whose last access was before a certain date.

3.7 Convert the following algorithm to an iterative form

```
function hcf (n, m : integer) : integer;
begin
if m > n then hcf := hcf(m,n)
else
if m = 0 then hcf := n
else
hcf := hcf(m, rem(n, m))
end;
```

3.8 Specify an implementation for a search package which fits the following constraints

(1) the directory maps integers (range 0 to 9999) into unbounded alphanumeric character strings (of average length 25 characters);

(2) the efficient retrieval of character strings is of high importance whereas accessing the directory entries in numerical order is of low importance;

(3) the directory will never contain more than 150 entries and once constructed it will only be subject to a few insertions and deletions;

(4) the machine on which the package is to be implemented has (i) 16-bit words, (ii) no multiply/divide hardware, (iii) 4K words are available for the storage structure (that is, directory excluding routines).

3.9 Design the necessary algorithms for a variation of the overflow with chaining hashing method which uses linked binary search trees instead of linear linked lists to store the overflow entries.

3.10 The set of permutations of N symbols can be generated by taking each symbol in turn and prefixing it to all permutations which result from the remaining $N - 1$ symbols. Design a recursive permutation generator algorithm that uses this approach.

3.11 (Sussenguth, 1963) A general tree differs from a binary tree in that it may have a variable number of subtrees. However, any general trees can be represented by a binary tree using a correspondence rule. Let $t_0, t_1, t_2, \ldots$, be general trees and $bt_0, bt_1, bt_2, \ldots$, be their binary tree representation. The correspondence may be stated as

(a)   if t_1 is the first or leftmost subtree of t_0 then bt_1 is the left subbinary tree of bt_0

(b)   if t_1 and t_2 are two brother subtrees (in that order) then bt_2 is the right subbinary tree of bt_1.

Give the corresponding binary trees for the figure.

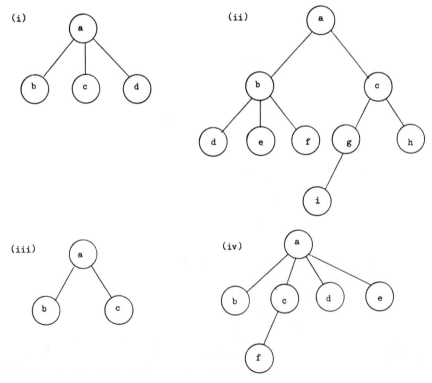

Figure Exercise 3.11

3.12 A general tree (exercise 3.11) may be used as the structure for a search directory, for example, the directory with keys

{BAN, BEAT, BOA, BOAR, BOAT, CARD, CART}

could be structured as shown in the figure.

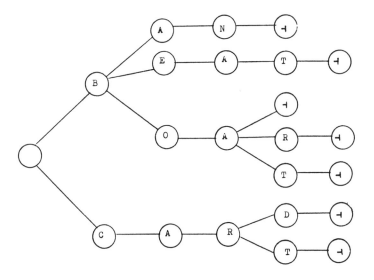

⊣ is the word terminator.

Figure Exercise 3.12

(a)   What is the value of the average search length for the directory shown above?
(b)   Outline a locate algorithm for such directories.
(c)   Draw the equivalent binary tree for the above binary tree.
(d)   Define the search algorithm (b) in terms of binary search tree operations only.

3.13 A doubly recursive definition of the factorial function can be developed using the following relationship factorial$(n) = f(n,1) = f(n,n \textbf{ div } 2 + 1)$ * $f(n \textbf{ div } 2,1)$. Complete the definition of factorial(n) and produce the corresponding recursive function. Transform this function to an iterative form.

3.14 A *complete* binary tree is one with all levels filled, except possibly the last, and this last level is filled from the leftmost position. Show that it is possible to implement a complete binary tree without using pointers or links.

3.15 Design a suitable implementation for each of the following array structures and give algorithms for accessing the array elements.

(a) a : **array** $[1 .. n]$ **of** string
(b) a : **array** $[0 .. 30, 0 .. 30]$ **of** real
       where $a[i,j] = -a[j,i]$ if $j \neq i$.
(c) a : **array** $[10 .. 20, 0 .. 20]$ **of** real
       where $a[i,j] \neq 0$ iff $i \geqslant j$.

14 *Designing Programs from Data Structures*

14.1 INTRODUCTION

Dijkstra (1973) has remarked that to the processing unit of a computer, the sequence of millions of program instructions it performs in a short period of time is extremely monotonous: it just performs instructions one after the other. He proceeds to explain that if we dare to interpret the whole happening as meaningful, it is only because we have mentally grouped sequences of instructions in such a way, that we can distinguish a structure in the whole happening. In other words we can say the structure of an object is really how an observer (processor) relates to that object; to give meaning to an amorphous sequence of instructions or data, the rules governing its structure have to be known. In the case of data, it is type that defines and expresses structure.

The data structures that appear in 'well-structured' programs do so because of their relevance to the problem being solved, that is, they model some feature of the outside world. Our programs may therefore be regarded as transforming structures. Externally represented structures are input, converted to internal form, whereupon they are processed until at some point they are output in external form. By identifying and defining the structured types to be processed we produce more transparent and reliable programs and in some cases, we can get an additional benefit of being able to derive the algorithm almost directly from the type structure definitions. The derivation is particularly simple when the mapping between two types is a function that can be realised by a composition of sequential processing and simple substitution.

14.2 TRAVERSING BINARY TREES

As a simple example of the derivation of algorithms from structure definitions, consider the systematic traversal of binary trees. Algorithms which 'visit' all the items of a binary tree are the basis of algorithms for operations on binary trees that involve performing the same suboperation on all items. Typical of this class of operations is printing all items of a binary tree.

It follows from the abstract definition of the binary tree type *T*

rectype *T* = **record**
        case tag : (empty, nonempty) of
        empty : ( );
        nonempty : **record**
                left : *T*;
                value : item type;
                right : *T*
                end;
      end

that there are three components of a non-empty binary tree to be visited and they may be visited in 3! different orderings. Three of these orderings are more frequently encountered than the others and we shall concentrate on them.

(1)   *Preorder* or depth first: Visit binary tree *t* in the order *t*.value, *t*.left, *t*.right (figure 14.1).

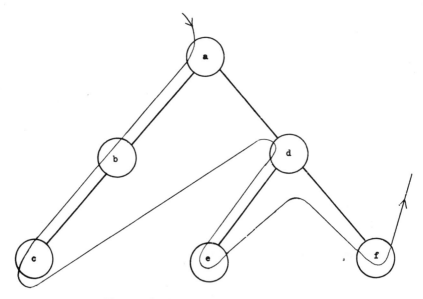

Figure 14.1 Preorder traversal = a b c d e f

(2)   *Postorder*: Visit binary tree *t* in the order *t*.left, *t*.value, *t*.right (figure 14.2).

(3)   *Endorder*: Visit binary tree *t* in order *t*.left, *t*.right, *t*.value (figure 14.3).
    The names pre-, post-, and endorder come from the order of *t*.value relative to the two subtrees of *t*. Because these orderings treat a binary tree as a sequence of three components, two of which are themselves binary trees, we may construct recursive traversal algorithms directly from the type definition.

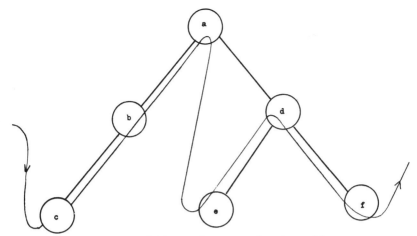

Figure 14.2 Postorder traversal = c b a e d f

For example, preorder traversal can be written as

procedure preorder(*p* : ↑ **binarytree of** item);
      begin
      case *p* ↑ .tag : (empty, nonempty) **of**
      empty   : ;   {do nothing}
      nonempty : **begin**
                 print   (*p* ↑ .value);   {visit *p* ↑ .value}
                 preorder (@(*p* ↑ .left));
                 preorder (@(*p* ↑ .right))
               end
    end
    end

The other two orderings can be obtained by permuting the three statements of
the non-empty case. They may be made more efficient by eliminating calls when
the subtree is empty; for example

procedure endorder (*p* : ↑ **binarytree of** item);
      begin   {*p* ↑ must be nonempty binary tree}
      if *p* ↑ .left.tag ≠ empty **then** endorder (@(*p* ↑ .left));
      if *p* ↑ .right.tag ≠ empty **then** endorder (@(*p* ↑ .right));
      print (*p*↑ .value);
    end

Iterative versions of these algorithms can be constructed using a stack as
considered in chapter 12. As presented, these algorithms will print the items of
the binary tree in the desired order, but without the inclusion of punctuation
characters it is not possible to recreate the binary tree from whence they came.
For example, the preorder sequence of values '*abcdef*' can come from any of
the binary trees shown in figure 14.4.

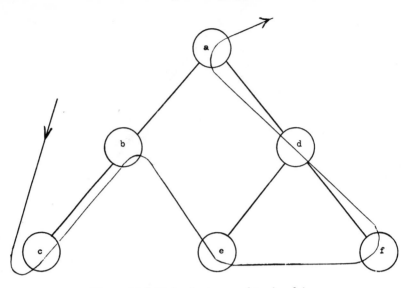

Figure 14.3 Endorder traversal = c b e f d a

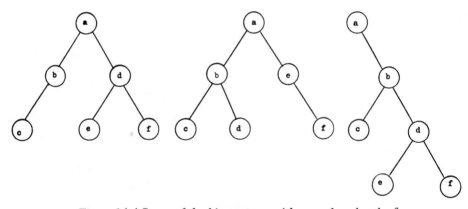

Figure 14.4 Some of the binary trees with preorder a b c d e f

The algorithms can be simply modified to include punctuation so as to show the binary tree structure in a one-dimensional form

```
procedure postorder (p : ↑ binarytree of item);
      begin    {p ↑ must be a nonempty binary tree}
      print ('(');
      if p ↑ .left.tag ≠ empty then postorder (@(p ↑ .left));
      print (',',p ↑ .value,',');
      if p ↑ .right.tag ≠ empty then postorder (@(p ↑ .right));
      print (')');
      end
```

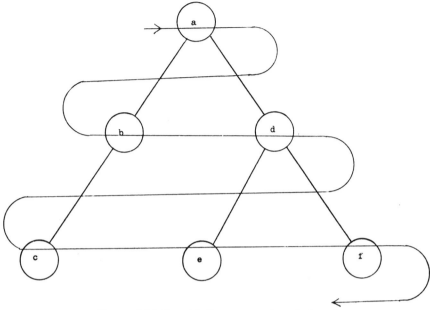

Figure 14.5 Breadth first traversal = a b d c e f

We can also traverse binary trees in ways that ignore the binary tree structure definition. The most important of these is known as *breadth first*, in which the traversal starts from the root and works down the binary tree, level by level, visiting all the nodes on the same level in a left to right fashion (figure 14.5).

The definition of breadth first traversal, in terms of levels, clashes with the definition of binary trees, which is in terms of subtrees. Consequently we cannot derive the algorithm from the structure definition. Resorting to intuition we notice that on reaching a node we visit it, then any nodes to the right of it on the same level, and then its left and right sons. The following algorithm achieves this ordering by use of a queue structure.

```
procedure breadthfirst (p : ↑ binarytree of item);
    var t : ↑ binarytree of item;
        q :   queue of (↑ binarytree of item);
    begin
    q.init;
    q.enter (p);
    while not q.empty do
        begin
        t := q.get;
        print (t ↑ .value);   {visit t ↑ .value}
        if t ↑ .left.tag ≠ empty then q.enter (@(t ↑ .left));
        if t ↑ .right.tag ≠ empty then q.enter (@(t ↑ .right));
        end
    end;
```

The maximum length of the queue is determined by the number of items and shape of the binary tree. A well balanced and complete binary tree with $2^n - 1$ nodes, has a bottom level with 2^{n-1} nodes. Therefore for a binary tree with m nodes the queue will reach a maximum length of at most (m **div** $2 + 1$) entries.

Breadth first traversal would appear to have no simple recursive algorithm since the iterative algorithm requires a queue rather than a stack. This algorithm can be used as the basis of a controlled search of a binary tree if there is some priority value attached to each item, all that has to be done is to reorder the queue, according to priority, before each get operation.

14.3 INPUT OF ADVANCED DATA STRUCTURES

A problem that frequently arises in connection with dynamic data structures is how to represent them externally, and how to design a procedure to transform the chosen external textual form into the internal representation. Even when an input procedure is not needed as a component of the final program, the availability of one often greatly reduces the time and effort involved in program testing. In contrast, as the last section illustrated, output is often very simple and will not be considered further.

As an example of the difficulties involved in inputting a dynamic data structure, consider the polynomials of two variables used in the symbolic addition procedure of chapter 9. The intuitive approach to designing an external form for such structures is to specify that everything has, as far as possible, a fixed format, that is, all components should either be of fixed length or have unique terminators, etc. In the case of polynomials we might require all coefficients and exponents to be explicit, allowing no default values and, further to reduce program complexity, we might restrict the use of spaces to exactly one before and after each term. Thus the polynomial

$$7x^3 y^5 + 2x^2 + xy^2 - 7$$

would have to be typed or punched as

$$\nabla 7X\uparrow 3Y\uparrow 5 \nabla + \nabla 2X\uparrow 2Y\uparrow 0 \nabla + \nabla 1X\uparrow 1Y\uparrow 2 \nabla - \nabla 7X\uparrow 0Y\uparrow 0 \nabla$$

Such a format is unpleasant and inconvenient to use and, because of its rigidity, is extremely susceptible to being mistyped. It is natural therefore to desire a more flexible format for the input. The increased variety possible in the input means that the recognising procedure has to be more complex, which in turn makes it a non-trivial task to test that all valid inputs are handled correctly.

Essentially the problem is that of 'compiling' the polynomials into a suitable data structure. It seems reasonable therefore to borrow the tools and methods of the compiler writer for our task of defining, recognising and processing external structures.

The *syntax*, or set of strings belonging to a programming language can be rigorously defined using Backus—Naur Form (BNF) notation. The syntax is defined by a *grammar*, which is a series of equations known as *productions*. The right-hand side of each production defines the set of strings belonging to the BNF variable (an identifier enclosed in ⟨,⟩ brackets) on the left-hand side. The right-hand side itself is a combination of BNF variables, terminals (symbols belonging to the alphabet of the language being defined) and operators. The basic BNF operators are

       concatention   .   'followed by'
       alternation | 'or'

which we extend to include

       iteration (Kleene star)   *   'zero or more occurrences of'

and the use of brackets (,) to indicate the priority of operators.

Using BNF, a convenient syntax for polynomials is

⟨polynomial⟩	::= [.space*.(⟨term⟩.space*)*.]
⟨term⟩	::= ⟨sign⟩.space*.⟨coefficient⟩.⟨exponents⟩
⟨sign⟩	::= + | −
⟨coefficients⟩	::= ⟨unsigned integer⟩|⟨empty⟩
⟨exponents⟩	::= ((X. ↑ .⟨integer⟩)|⟨empty⟩).
	((Y. ↑ .⟨integer⟩)|⟨empty⟩)
⟨integer⟩	::= ((⟨sign⟩.⟨unsigned integer⟩)|⟨unsigned integer⟩)
⟨unsigned integer⟩	::= ⟨digit⟩⟨digit⟩*
⟨empty⟩	::=

This syntax allows a fairly free format for polynomials. Each polynomial is delimited by the use of [,] brackets. Spaces may occur anywhere, except between a coefficient and exponent of a term. All terms, including the first, must be preceded by a sign. Coefficients may be omitted, and so may be exponents to the power zero, but there is no default for $X ↑ 1$ or $Y ↑ 1$. Thus the polynomial shown above could be input as

$$[\nabla+\nabla\nabla7X ↑ 3Y ↑ 5\nabla+\nabla\nabla2X ↑ 2\nabla+\nabla X ↑ 1Y ↑ 2\nabla-\nabla7]$$

The BNF grammar also permits as valid inputs some strings which we might reasonably wish to exclude. For example, the grammar allows as polynomials strings such as

$$[\nabla+\nabla]$$

which are quite obviously nonsense. Such inputs can be excluded by making the grammar, and hence its recognising procedure, more complex. The extent to which it is worth while making the changes to exclude 'incorrect' inputs depends on the likely frequency of such errors occurring and the damage caused if they do occur. In a compiler such checks are clearly essential, in a one-off input procedure for limited use as a test driver, they are probably not.

The BNF productions may be used to produce a recogniser program, in which each production becomes a procedure to recognise the defined BNF variable. We assume that at all times the currently scanned input terminal is available in the variable rec; the procedure get is used to assign to rec the value of the next input symbol when the processing of the current one has been completed. The right-hand side of each production is used to construct procedures as follows.

Each terminal in the production is checked using an **if then else** statement; variables become calls on the appropriate recognising procedure. Alternatives are tested by **if** statements; and iterations become **while** loops, the conditions in both cases being formed by tests for the first symbol(s) of the alternative or iteration. Thus the recogniser for polynomial is

```
procedure polynomial;
        begin    {⟨polynomial⟩ ::= [.space*.(⟨term⟩.space*)*.]}
        if rec ≠ '[' then error
                        else get;
        skipspaces;
        while signs.has(rec)do    {a +, − must start ⟨term⟩}
                begin
                term;
                skipspaces
                end
        if rec ≠ ']' then error
                        else get
        end
```

where **const** signs = (+, −) and **procedure** skipspaces is used recognise space*

```
procedure skipspaces;
        const space = ' ';
        begin
        while rec = space do get
        end;
```

and error is a call on a procedure to be invoked in the event of an error condition. Recognisers can be instructed for the other non-terminals in a similar manner.

```
procedure term;
        begin    {⟨term⟩ ::= ⟨sign⟩.space*.⟨coefficient⟩.⟨exponents⟩}
        sign;
        skipspaces;
        coefficient;
        exponents
        end;
procedure sign;
        begin    {⟨sign⟩ ::= + | −}
        if rec = '+' or rec = '−' then get
                                else error
        end;
```

procedure coefficient;
      begin   {⟨coefficient⟩ ::= ⟨unsigned integer⟩|⟨empty⟩}
      if digits.has(rec) **then** unsigned int
      end

where the global constant digits is defined by

    const digits = ('0','1','2','3','4','5','6','7','8','9')
        procedure exponents;
            begin {⟨exponents⟩ ::= ((X. ↑ ⟨integer⟩))|⟨empty⟩).
                                   ((Y. ↑ ⟨integer⟩)|⟨empty⟩)
          if rec = 'X' **then begin**
                  get;
                  if rec = '↑' **then begin**
                            get;
                            integer
                            end
                       else error
                end;
          if rec = 'Y' **then begin**
                  get;
                  if rec = '↑' **then begin**
                            get;
                            integer
                            end
                       else error
                end;
        end
      procedure integer;
          begin   {⟨integer⟩ ::= (⟨sign⟩.⟨unsigned integer⟩)|⟨unsigned
                                                    integer⟩}
          if rec = '+' **or** rec = '−' **then** get;
          unsignedint
          end
      procedure unsignedint;
          begin   {⟨unsigned integer⟩ ::= ⟨digit⟩ ⟨digit⟩*}
          if digits.has(rec) **then**
              begin
              get;
              while digits.has(rec) **do** get
              end
          else error
          end;

To ensure that rec initially contains the first input symbol, there must be an initial call on get before the first call on polynomial.

The correctness of the recognising procedures can be informally verified, since their structure is directly related to the structure of the defining productions. The procedures may now be used as the framework for the program to construct an internal representation of polynomials. This is analogous to the method of compiler construction, known as 'recursive descent', in which the code generation statements are inserted into the syntax analysis routines.

```
procedure readpoly (var r : ↑ sequence of term);
        var s : ↑ sequence of term;
            t : term;
        begin {⟨polynomial⟩ ::= [.space*.(⟨term⟩.space*)*.]}
        if rec ≠ '[' then error
                    else get;
        s ↑ .init;
        skipspaces;
        while signs.has(rec)
            do begin
                readterm (t);
                if t.coeff ≠ 0 then s ↑ .addend(t);
                skipspaces
                end;
        if rec ≠ '[' then error else get;
        r := s
        end;
procedure readterm (var t : term);
        var s : signs;
        begin    {⟨terms⟩ : := ⟨sign⟩.space *.⟨coefficient⟩.⟨exponents⟩}
        readsign(s);
        skipspaces;
        readcoeff (t.coeff);
        readexps (t.exp);
        if t.coeff = 0 and t.exp ≠ exponenttype (0,0) then t.coeff = 1;
        if s = '−' then t.coeff := −t.coeff;
        end;
procedure readsign (var s : signs);
        begin    {⟨sign⟩ : := + | −}
        if rec = '+' then begin
                            s := '+';
                            get
                            end
        else
        if rec = '−' then begin
                            s := '−'
                            get
                            end
```

```
        else error
        end;
procedure readcoeff (var i : integer);
     begin   {⟨coefficient⟩ : := ⟨unsigned integer⟩|⟨empty⟩}
     if digits.has(rec) then readunsignedint(i);
     end;
procedure readexps (var e : exponentype);
     begin   {⟨exponents⟩ : := ((X. ↑ .⟨integer⟩|⟨empty⟩).
                              ((Y. ↑ .⟨integer⟩|⟨empty⟩)
     e := exponentype (0,0);
     if rec = 'X' then begin
                 get;
                 if rec = '↑' then begin
                             get;
                             readinteger(e.xexp)
                             end
                             else error
                 end;
     if rec = 'Y' then begin
                 get;
                 if rec = '↑' then begin
                             get;
                             readinteger(e.yexp)
                             end
                         else error
                 end
     end;
procedure readinteger (var val : integer);
     var sign : (−1. . + 1);   {−1 = neg, +1 = pos}
     begin   {⟨integer⟩ : := ⟨sign⟩⟨unsigned integer⟩|⟨unsigned integer⟩}
     sign := +1;   {default for no sign}
     if rec = '+' then get
     else
     if rec = '−' then begin
                   sign := −1;
                   get
                   end
     readunsignedint(val);
     val := sign*val
     end
procedure readunsignedint (var val : integer)
     var v : integer;
     begin   {⟨unsigned integer⟩ : := ⟨digit⟩⟨digit⟩}
     if digits.has(rec) then
          begin
```

```
            v := integer val(rec);   {integer value of digit char}
            get;
            while digits.has(rec)
                    do begin
                            v := 10*v + integerval(rec);
                            get
                            end
                end
            else error
        end;
```

   The technique used to design the read polynomial procedures is to be
recommended on account of the high degree of faith we may have in the
resulting programs. Breaking the construction into the three phases: define input
syntax, construct the recogniser, insert processing statements, means we can
concentrate on the essentially separate issues involved in each of the phases.
Furthermore we can conveniently check the correctness of the program, as it is
constructed, at the end of each phase.
   The reliability of the resultant program can be further enhanced if we ensure
that we only use a restricted type of BNF grammars.
   In that case we can use a set of program construction rules 'mechanically' to
produce the recogniser program. To prove the correctness of a recogniser
produced using the rules, we only have to check that the rules have been applied
correctly; this is considerably simpler than proving program correctness.

14.4 PROGRAM CONSTRUCTION RULES (Wirth, 1975)

The task of recognising an input string is simplified, if, whenever we are faced by
a choice during the recognition process, the choice can be made without having
to read ahead beyond the current input symbol. This simplification is possible
for grammar satisfying the following two restrictions.
Restriction 1   Consider a production of the form

$$\langle A \rangle : = \alpha_1 \,|\alpha_2\,|\,\ldots\,|\alpha_n$$

to decide solely on the contents of rec, which if any of the alternatives are
present, all the terminals that may be the first symbol of a string derived from α_i
must be distinct from the set of first strings derived from any other α_j. More
formally

$$\text{first } (\alpha_i) \cap \text{first } (\alpha_j) = \varnothing \qquad \text{for } i \neq j$$

where first (α_i) is the set of all terminal symbols that can appear in the first
position of strings derived from α_i.
   In the grammar for polynomials we only have to consider the following
productions

⟨sign⟩　　　　: := +ₗ| −
⟨coefficient⟩ : := ⟨unsigned integer⟩|⟨empty⟩
⟨exponents⟩ : := ((X. .⟨integer⟩|⟨empty⟩).
　　　　　　　　((Y. .⟨integer⟩|⟨empty⟩)
⟨integer⟩　　: := ⟨sign⟩⟨unsigned integer⟩|⟨unsigned integer⟩

since they are the only ones involving alternatives. The restriction is not violated, since each alternative within a production has a distinct set of initial symbols.
Restriction 2　A problem also occurs when trying to match the current input symbol against a variable, ⟨A⟩ say, which can produce the empty string. The value of rec must be sufficient to specify whether the empty or non-empty alternative of ⟨A⟩ is present. Fₒᵣ this to be true the first symbols of any string that can follow ⟨A⟩ must be distinct from the first symbols of ⟨A⟩ itself. More formally, we require

first (⟨A⟩) ∩ follow (⟨A⟩) = ∅

where the set follow (⟨A⟩) is constructed by considering all productions, p_i, with alternatives of the form

$⟨X_i⟩$: := $α_i.⟨A⟩.β_i$

where $α_i, β_i$ are possibly empty strings of terminals and variables. The set follow (⟨A⟩) is the union of all the sets first $(β_i)$, and if $β_i$ can generate the empty set, then follow (⟨X_i⟩) must be included in follow ⟨A⟩ as well.

As a corollary of this rule it must be remembered that a starred variable or terminal $(β)^*$, can generate the empty set. Thus for example if we have a production of the form

$⟨A⟩$: := $α.(β)^*. γ$

we must have

first$(β)$ ∩ first$(γ)$ = ∅

and furthermore if we can derive the empty set from γ then we must also have

first$(β)$ ∩ follow$(⟨A⟩)$ = ∅

The values of first and follow are tabulated below for each of the variables of the polynomial grammar.

variable	$\overset{*}{\Rightarrow}$ ⟨empty⟩	first	follow
⟨polynomial⟩	no	[	⟨empty⟩
⟨term⟩	no	+,−	space,+,−,]
⟨sign⟩	no	+,−	space digit,X,Y,+,−,]
⟨coefficient⟩	yes	⟨digit⟩	X,Y,space,+,−,]
⟨exponents⟩	yes	X,Y	space,+,−,]
⟨integer⟩	no	+,−,digit	Y,space,] ,+,−

As can be seen, restriction 2 is satisfied because

$$\text{first} (\langle\text{coefficient}\rangle) \cap \text{follow} (\langle\text{coefficient}\rangle) = \varnothing$$
$$\text{first} (\langle\text{exponents}\rangle) \cap \text{follow} (\langle\text{exponents}\rangle) = \varnothing$$

The purpose of these restrictions is to simplify the process of recognition, to the extent that the recognising program can be constructed algorithmically using the following set of construction rules. As before, the input is read by a procedure get, which assigns the value of the next input symbol to the global variable, rec. The recogniser for α, terminal symbol or variable, is denoted by $p(\alpha)$.

Rule 1

For productions of the form

$$\langle\alpha\rangle : = \alpha_1 \cdot \alpha_2 \cdot \ldots \cdot \alpha_n$$

where α_i may be a terminal or a variable

$p(\langle\alpha\rangle)$ is **begin**
    $p(\alpha_1)$;
    $p(\alpha_2)$;

    .
    .
    .

    $p(\alpha_n)$
    end

Rule 2

For productions of the form

$$\langle\alpha\rangle : = \alpha_1 \mid \alpha_2 \mid \ldots \mid \alpha_n$$

where α_i may be a terminal or a variable

$p(\langle\alpha\rangle)$ is **if** first (α_1).has(rec) **then** $p(\alpha_1)$
    else
    if first (α_2).has(rec) **then** $p(\alpha_2)$
    else

    .
    .
    .

    if first (α_n).has(rec) **then** $p(\alpha_n)$
    else
    error

Rule 3

For productions of the form

$$\langle\alpha\rangle : = (\alpha_1)^*$$

where α_1 may be a terminal or a variable then

$p(\langle\alpha\rangle)$ is **while** first (α_1).has(rec) **do** $p(\alpha_1)$

Rule 4

If α is a terminal symbol then

$p(\langle\alpha\rangle)$ is **if** rec = α **then** get **else** error

Rule 5

If α is a variable then $p(\alpha)$ is a call of a procedure constructed using these rules.

Rule 6

The recogniser for the entire grammar, $\langle\beta\rangle$, must be embedded in a framework

> **begin**
> get;
> $p(\langle\beta\rangle)$
> **end**

Since the polynomial grammar is a single symbol lookahead grammar, the recognising procedures, which were presented earlier as being produced intuitively, were in fact constructed 'mechanically' using the program construction rules. Though, quite naturally, certain obvious redundancies have been removed.

In cases, where a grammar is not single symbol lookahead, it is worth attempting to transform it into an equivalent grammar that is. But it should be borne in mind that the transformation is not always possible without modifying the language being defined.

14.5 SYSTEMATIC DESIGN OF FILE PROCESSING PROGRAMS

The method of design outlined in the previous section can also be applied to the design of certain file processing applications programs. The traditional data processing sequential file can be defined by a BNF grammar, therefore where the output file is a straight match of the input file we can construct the program by constructing a recogniser and inserting the appropriate output statements.

To show the technique in practice it is applied to the following program specification for a file report program. The program is a simplified version of one of a suite of programs for maintaining an outstanding orders system for a college bursar's department.

Example

The program suite maintains an Outstanding Order Master File which contains all the transactions (that is, the original order and all relevant invoices, credit notes and cancellations) pertaining to each purchase order made by the college that is yet to be completed. The purpose of our program is to print a report of the contents of this file. The masterfile consists of a single record for each order, invoice, credit note or cancellation, each record contains

(1)   the value, type, and reference number of the transaction (and in the case of orders a description of the goods is carried); it also carries information such as

(2)   the nominal code (that is, college department number) to which the transaction applies, the order number of the original order, and the date of the transaction.

The file is sorted in ascending order on order number, nominal code and date. Our report program has to print out the contents of the whole file with the outstanding order value shown for every order and for every nominal code within each order. The outstanding value is the sum of the original order value plus the contents of this field in any invoices, cancellations, and credit notes.

   The first task is to obtain a syntactic definition of the outstanding order master file (⟨oomfile⟩), which we note consists of a series of sequences of records pertaining to the same order number (⟨ordernoseq⟩), followed by an end of file (eof) record

$$\langle \text{oomfile} \rangle : = (\langle \text{ordernoseq} \rangle)^* . \text{eof} \tag{1}$$

Proceeding in a top-down manner we may define ⟨ordernoseq⟩ by

$$\langle \text{ordernoseq} \rangle : = \text{neworderno}.\langle \text{nomseqtail} \rangle.(\text{newnomcode}.\langle \text{nomseqtail} \rangle)^* \tag{2}$$

where

neworderno	is a record with a different (greater than) order number from its predecessor. This record also introduces a new nominal code and date for the purposes of sequence checking.
newnomcode	is a record with the same order number as the previous neworderno record, but with a greater than nominal code. This record introduces a new date for the purposes of sequence checking.
⟨nomseqtail⟩	is a sequence of records all with the same order number as the last neworderno record and the same nominal code as the previous neworderno or newnomcode record depending on which came last.

Similarly we can define

$$\langle \text{nomseqtail} \rangle : = \langle \text{dateseqtail} \rangle.(\text{newdate}.\langle \text{dateseqtail} \rangle)^* \tag{3}$$

where

> newdate   is a record with the same order number as the last
> neworderno record and the same nominal code as the
> previous neworderno or newnomcode but it has a different
> date from its predecessor. It introduces a new date for the
> purposes of sequence checking.
>
> ⟨dateseqtail⟩   is a sequence of records all with the same order number,
> nominal code and date.

Finally we can define

$$⟨\text{dateseqtail}⟩ : = (\text{samedate})^* \tag{4}$$

where

> samedate   is a record with the same order number, nominal code and
> date as its predecessor.

Clearly {neworderno, newnomcode, newdate, samedate, eof} constitute an 'alphabet' of basic record types and the file may be described by either the BNF productions (1) to (4) or by a regular expression obtained by substitution.

> (neworder.(samedate)*.(newdate.(samedate)*)*.(newnomcode.(samedate)*
> (newdate.(samedate)*)*)*)*.eof

The set of productions is simpler to work from than a single production with the regular expression as its right-hand side.

Using the program construction rules given above we can generate a parser program for the outstanding order master file.

To use the rules we need a procedure read which gets the next record in the file together with the record type (that is, which of the basic types neworder, newnomcode, newdate, samedate or eof it is).

We also introduce a special rule (rule 7) to deal solely with ⟨file⟩ definitions; it can be derived from rules 1 to 6.

Rule 7

For production of the form

$$⟨α⟩ : = (α_1)^*.\text{eof}$$

where $α_1$ is a terminal or a variable and eof the special terminal record marking end of file

> $p(⟨α⟩)$ is **while** rec ≠ eof
>   **do** $p(α_1)$

Note that this rule leaves rec still containing eof and unlike the other rules not the next record to be processed.

The program represents a less redundant version of the one derived by completely mechanical application of the construction rules.

```
var rec : (neworderno, newnomcode, newdate, samedate, eof);
                                           {alphabet of record types}
procedure p(⟨ordernoseq⟩);
    begin   {⟨ordernoseq⟩ : := neworderno.⟨nomseqtail⟩.
                              (newnomcode.⟨nomseqtails⟩)*}
    if rec ≠ neworderno then error    {rules 3,4}
                        else get
    p(⟨nomseqtail⟩);
    while rec = newnomcode do begin    {rules 3,4}
                            get;
                            p(⟨nomseqtail⟩);
                            end
    end;
procedure p(⟨nomseqtail⟩);    {rules 3,4}
    begin   {⟨nomseqtail⟩ : := ⟨dateseqtail⟩.(newdate.⟨dateseqtail⟩)*}
    p(⟨dateseqtail⟩);
    while rec = newdate do begin
                        get;
                        p(⟨dateseqtail⟩)
                        end
    end
procedure p(⟨dateseqtail⟩);
    begin   {⟨dateseqtail⟩ : := (samedate)*}
    while rec = samedate do get    {rule 3}
    end;
begin {⟨oomfile⟩ : := (⟨ordernoseq⟩)*.eof}
get;
while rec ≠ eof do p(⟨ordernoseq⟩)}    {rules 6,7}
end;
```

The next stage is to discover the necessary processing and output statements and relate them to the syntactic structure of the input file.

An analysis of the problem and the desired output file reveals that

(1)   every input record has to be output
(2)   after every ⟨ordernoseq⟩ has been recognised the total of order values for that ⟨ordernoseq⟩ has to be output
(3)   after every neworderno.⟨nomseqtail⟩ and after every newnomcode.⟨nomseqtail⟩ has been recognised the total of order values for that sequence has to be output.

In addition, an initial heading line and final last line should be printed. The only processing to be done is for the summation of the order values for each order number sequence and nominal code number sequence. The abstract program is therefore

```
var rec : (neworderno, newnomcode, newdate, samedate, eof);
    ordernoseqtotal, nomcodeseqtotal : integer;
procedure p'(⟨ordernoseq⟩);
    begin    {⟨ordernoseq⟩ : := neworderno.⟨nomseqtail⟩.(newnomcode.
                                                    ⟨nomseqtail⟩)*}
        if rec ≠ neworderno then error
                            else begin
                                    printneworderline (rec);
                                    initialise (ordernoseqtotal);
                                    initialise (nomcodeseq total);
                                    process (rec);
                                    get
                                    end;
        p'(⟨nomseqtail⟩);
        while rec = newnomcode do begin
                                    print newnomcode line (rec);
                                    initialise (nomseqcodeseq total);
                                    process (rec);
                                    get;
                                    p'(⟨nomseqtail⟩);
                                    end;
        print order-number sequence total line
        end;
procedure p'(⟨nomseqtail⟩);
    begin    {⟨nomseqtail⟩ : := ⟨dateseqtail⟩.(newdate.⟨dateseqtail⟩)*}
        p'(⟨dateseqtail⟩);
        while rec = newdate do begin
                                    print same nomcode line (rec);
                                    process (rec);
                                    get;
                                    p'(⟨dateseqtail⟩)
                                    end;
        print nom-code sequence total-line;
        end;
procedure p'(⟨dateseqtail⟩);
    begin    {⟨dateseqtail⟩ : := (samedate)*}
        while rec = samedate do begin
                                    print same nomcode line (rec);
                                    process (rec);
                                    get
                                    end
```

```
    end;
    begin    {oomfile} : := (⟨ordernoseq⟩)*.eof}
    print heading
    get
    while rec ≠ eof do p'(⟨ordernoseq⟩);
    print lastline
    end
```

The initialise and process procedures are defined by the operations required on individual records. In this case quite clearly initialise merely sets to zero the parameter, and process adds in the order value of the current records. Thus

```
procedure initialise (var x : integer);
    begin
    x := 0;
    end
```

and

```
procedure process (rec);
    begin
    ordernoseqtotal := ordernoseq total + rec.value;
    nomcodeseqtotal := nomcodeseq total + rec.value
    end
```

In this example and in general, the record processing aspects (initialise and process) are textually separate from the file processing aspects, because they are dealt with separately by the design method. This is to be welcomed because it allows a change in file structure to be made to the program without necessitating a redesign of the record processing aspects (and vice versa).

The remaining task is to code the design into a suitable program language. In the real world a suitable language for this problem will usually mean Cobol, and hence a Cobol procedure division equivalent of the design is given

```
BØDY-ØF-PRØGRAM.
    PERFØRM  PRINT-HEADINGS.
    PERFØRM-READ-ØRDER-MASTER-FILE-REC.
    PERFØRM  PRØCESS-ØRDER-NØ-SEQ  UNTIL
    ØRDER-MASTER-FILE-EØF.
    PERFØRM  PRINT-LAST-LINE.
PRØCESS-ØRDER-NØ-SEQ.
    IF  NEW-ØRDER-NØ-REC
        PERFØRM  PRINT-NEW-ØRDER-LINE
        MØVE  O  TØ  ØRDER-NØ-SEQ-VALUE-TØTAL
        MØVE  O  TØ  NØM-CØDE-SEQ-VALUE-TØTAL
        PERFØRM  PRØCESS-ØRDER-MASTER-REC
        PERFØRM  READ-ØRDER-MASTER-FILE-REC
```

```
          ELSE  GØ  TØ  ERRØR-1
      PERFØRM  PRØCESS-NØM-CØDE-SEQ-TAIL.
      PERFØRM  PRØCESS-NØM-CØDE-SEQ  UNTIL  NØT
          NEW-NØM-CØDE-REC.
      PERFØRM  PRINT-ØRDER-NØSEQ-TØTAL-LINE.
  PRØCESS-NØM-CØDE-SEQ.
      PERFØRM  PRINT-NEW-NØM-CØDE  LINE.
      MØVE  O  TØ  NØM-CØDE-SEQ-VALUE-TØTAL.
      PERFØRM  PRØCESS-ØRDER-MASTER-REC.
      PERFØRM  READ-ØRDER-MASTER-FILE.
      PERFØRM  PRØCESS-NØM-CØDE-SEQ-TAIL.
  PRØCESS-NØM-CØDE-SEQ-TAIL.
      PERFØRM  PRØCESS-DATE-SEQ-TAIL.
      PERFØRM  PRØCESS-DATE-SEQ  UNTIL  NØT  NEW-DATE-REC.
      PERFØRM  PRINT-NØM-CØDE-SEQ-TØTAL-LINE.
  PRØCESS-DATE-SEQ.
      PERFØRM  PRINT-SAME-NØM-CØDE-LINE.
      PERFØRM  PRØCESS-ØRDER-MASTER-REC.
      PERFØRM  READ-ØRDER-MASTER-FILE-REC.
      PERFØRM  PRØCESS-DATE-SEQ-TAIL.
  PRØCESS-DATE-SEQ-TAIL.
      PERFØRM  PRØCESS-SAME-DATE-REC  UNTIL
          NØT  SAME-DATE-REC.
  PRØCESS-SAME-DATE-REC.
      PERFØRM  PRINT-SAME-NØM-CØDE-LINE.
      PERFØRM  PRØCESS-ORDER-MASTER-REC.
      PERFØRM  READ-ØRDER-MASTER-FILE-REC.
```

In the above procedure division

while not condition **do** S;

is coded as the Cobol sentence

PERFØRM S UNTIL condition.

where condition is a level 88 condition name.

It must be stated that the design method does not provide a suitable technique for the design of all file processing programs, or indeed even for all single input file processing programs.

The complexity of the file structure determines whether the program construction rules can be applied. The complexity of the mapping between input and output files determines whether a program for the mapping can be produced directly from the parser.

To apply the construction rules the BNF must be capable of being recognised by single symbol lookahead. As an example of a structure requiring multiple symbol lookahead consider

⟨record-sequence⟩ : := ⟨good-seq⟩|⟨faulty-seq⟩
⟨good-seq⟩ : := (⟨record⟩)*.⟨good-indicator⟩
⟨faulty-seq⟩ : := (⟨record⟩)*.⟨faulty-indicator⟩

To distinguish between ⟨good-seq⟩ and ⟨faulty-seq⟩, the parser must be prepared to read (and save for processing) an indefinite number of ⟨record⟩s. In these situations we must resort to intuition.

To realise the mapping between input and output files, we construct what is essentially the equivalent of a finite state machine transducer between the input file and the output file. Consequently the method can only be used to construct mappings between input files and output files that can be realised by finite state machines. A theorem about the capabilities of finite state devices states the conditions which must be fulfilled if a function is to be realisable by a finite state machine. For practical purposes, where only sequential files are being considered, these conditions simplify to the following.

For a program to be capable of being designed by this method, the computed function f between input file and output file

(1)   must 'preserve' initial sequences of records of the input file, that is, if u is *any* initial sequence of records of the input file then $f(u)$ (the output from processing u) must be the initial sequence of records of the output file.

(2)   must have 'bounded outputs' for any sequence of records occurring in the input file, then there must be a fixed maximum number of records that can be output as the result of reading the next individual input record.

These two conditions debar us from using the method to design such programs as

(1)   A sort program. Consider an ascending order sort program and compare its actions on two files of integers $(6, 5, 4, 3)$ and $(6, 5, 4, 3, 2)$

$$f((6, 5, 4, 3)) = (3, 4, 5, 6)$$
$$f((6, 5, 4, 3, 2)) = (2, 3, 4, 5, 6)$$

This violates the preserve initial sequences condition and hence a sort program cannot be designed in this way.

(2)   A program to read the outstanding order master file and print it out iff it contains no cancellation records. This clearly violates the bounded outputs condition, no record can be printed until the whole file has been read (and there is no universal fixed bound on the length of the outstanding order master file).

Despite these limitations on the use of the method it is useful for that large class of problems where the data can be read and processed on a one item at a time basis. The method is a practical example of the *constructive approach* to program correctness and verification.

14.6 CONCLUSION

Basing program structure on the structure of data is not new — it has been used for years in compiler writing, as well as having been the basis of much of our intuition. It would seem, however, to be an area where much progress can be made along the road to making program development a rigorous and hence verifiable process. What remains to be tackled is the vast majority of problems which, for one reason or another, have no simple sequential relationship between input and output structures.

At the moment, stepwise refinement is still the best, general purpose, program design tool. However, other advances have been made, notably through the work of Jackson and Dijkstra. Michael Jackson, starting from a method similar to that used in this chapter, has developed a semi-rigorous method of classifying and dealing with input—output 'structure clashes'. Dijkstra's guarded commands constitute a calculus for program development such that if the rules of the calculus are followed, the correctness of the resulting program is guaranteed. The work of both these authors lies outside the scope of a book of this size, but the reader is recommended to read both Jackson's *Principles of Program Design* (1975) and Dijkstra's 'A Discipline of Programming' (1976).

14.7 SUMMARY

1. Structure is how an observer (processor) relates to an object.
2. For simple sequential functions on data structures, the algorithm can often be derived directly from the structure definition.
3. BNF can be used to define the external form of a structure.
4. Recognisers for single symbol lookahead grammars can be constructed by the use of a set of program construction rules.
5. Simple sequential file processing programs can be reliably developed using the program construction rules.

14.8 BIBLIOGRAPHICAL NOTES

The derivation of program structures from data structures as a program design technique was independently proposed by Jackson (1975) and Warnier (1974).

The use of Wirth's program construction rules as a design method is proposed in Coleman (1977a) on which section 14.5 is based. Also of interest in this respect is Coleman (1977b).

Exercises 4

4.1 The mailing list of a firm is stored as a file of records containing names and addresses. A name is a surname followed by a title (Mr, Ms, Dr, Prof.), followed by at least one initial (each initial is separated from its predecessor by a full stop). The address comprises a house number or house name, a street, a district or town, a city or county, and a postal code. Each field of the record is separated by a comma and a variable number of spaces

(a) Give a BNF definition of the input file (tightening up the above specification where necessary).
(b) Verify that the BNF definition is single symbol lookahead grammar.
(c) Design a program to print the records of the file as they should appear on address labels.

4.2 Consider the stock and transaction files specified in example 2 of chapter 5. Produce BNF definitions of these files and use them to design appropriate file report programs.

4.3 Give a BNF definition of the input data for exercise 1.9. Argue that the data cannot have a single symbol lookahead grammar definition. Show to what extent the BNF input definition is still useful as a program design aid.

4.4 Can the following problem be solved using the program construction rules? If not, why not? Design a solution to the problem.
  'A file consists of records each with a two digit identifying key. You are required to design a program to read the file and print out in order all those record keys which are not duplicated elsewhere on the file. For example, the output for input file record keys

  9, 52, 37, 9, 1, 26, 9, 37, 53

would be

  52, 1, 26, 53.'

4.5 If exercise 4.4 were changed to specify keys of type integer (where integers are in the range $\pm 2^{23}$), how would this affect your solution?

4.6 If exercise 4.4 were changed to require the output of the duplicate record keys, how would this affect your solution?

4.7 (Dijkstra, 1976) *Dutch National Flag Problem* There is a row of buckets numbered 1 through N. It is given that

(1)   each bucket contains one pebble,
(2)   each pebble is either red, white or blue.

A minicomputer is placed in front of this row of buckets and has to be programmed in such a way (if necessary) that the pebbles are in the order of the Dutch National Flag, that is, in order from low to high bucket number, first the red, then the white, and finally the blue pebbles. To be able to do so, the minicomputer has been equipped with one output command that enables it to interfere with pebble positions, namely

'bucketswap $(i,j)'$ for $1 \leqslant i \leqslant N$ and $1 \leqslant j \leqslant N$
for $i = j$ then pebbles left as they are
for $i \neq j$ then two computer controlled hands interchange the
        pebbles in buckets i and j

and one output command that can inspect the colour of a pebble, namely

'colour $(i)'$ for $1 \leqslant i \leqslant N$

A computer 'eye' is directed on bucket i and delivers the colour (red, white, or blue) of the pebble currently in the bucket.
The program

(a)   must be able to deal with all possible forms of missing colours,
(b)   the minicomputer has very small store and hence we are not allowed to introduce arrays of any sort,
(c)   the program may direct its 'eye' at most once on each pebble (the input operation is so time-consuming that looking twice at the same pebble would lead to an unacceptable loss of time).

(Hint: What is the connection between this problem and the partitioning required by quicksort?)

4.8 When planning a complex operation employing people and resources, the operation can normally be broken down into a number of activities, each requiring only some of the people and resources. Some of these activities can take place concurrently and some require others to be completed before they can be started. For example, building a house is broken into activities such as laying foundations, building walls, fitting windows, roofing, electric wiring, plastering, etc. Nothing can be done until the foundations have been laid; once the walls are completed, the roofing and fitting of windows can take place concurrently, etc. It is possible to estimate the time required for each activity and use this together with the necessary sequencing of activities to calculate the total time for the operation and to identify those activities where delay will increase the total times. Such activities are said to be critical and a sequence of critical activities each of which is dependent on the completion of the previous one and total duration is equal to the total time for the whole operation, is called a *critical path*.

Since the activities can be partially ordered, they can be represented by a directed graph with one first node, called the source and one last node, called the sink (see figure). Each edge represents an activity and the values on the edges the durations of each activity. The nodes are identified by numbers and represent events in time when all the activities incident *to* the node are completed and none of those incident *from* the node have started.

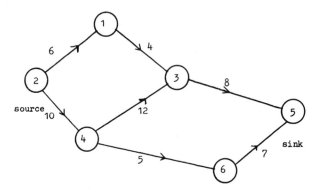

Figure Exercise 4.8

The paths from source to sink above are

     2, 1, 3, 5
     2, 4, 3, 5
     2, 4, 6, 5

Of these 2, 4, 3, 5 is critical and the total time for completion is 30 time units.

Non-critical events (nodes) are said to possess 'slack' and non-critical activities (edges) to have 'float', a number of different floats are identified. These are defined as follows

     slack (i) = LST (i) − EST (i)
     total float (i, j) = LST (j) − EST (i) − duration (i, j)

[This is the longest extra time that (i, j) can have without increasing the total duration of the operation.]

     free float (i, j) = EST (j) − EST (i) − duration (i, j)

[This is the longest extra time that (i, j) can have without delaying later activities.]

     independent float (i, j) = EST (j) − LST (i) − duration (i, j)

[This is the longest extra time that (i, j) can have independent of other activities exceeding their time] where EST (source) = 0, EST (i), $i \neq$ source = max (EST (j) + duration (j, i) $(j\ i)$ is and edge in the graph).

In the example above

slack (1) = 12 time units
slack (6) = 8 time units

	Total float	Free float	Independent float
(2, 1)	12	0	0
(1, 3)	12	12	0
(4, 6)	8	0	0
(6, 5)	8	8	0

Note In the example above, there is only one critical path, in general there may be more than one

You are required to design a program which will read in a weighted graph and print a critical path, the total time and the slack at each node.

The input should be in the form of

number of nodes
number of edges

A sequence of 'number of edges' triplets where each triplet, representing one edge consists of the node number of the end of the edge and the weight of the edge.

In the example above, the input would be

6; 7
2; 1; 6
1; 3; 4
2; 4; 10
4; 3; 12
3; 5; 8
4; 6; 5
6; 5; 7

and the output would be a listing of the inputs above followed by

CRITICAL PATH   2 4 3 5
TOTAL TIME   30
SLACK   1 12
                2 0
                3 0
                4 0
                5 0
                6 8

Method

As can be seen from the example output above, the critical path is a sequence of edges, the first of which is an activity which depends on no others, the last of which has no others depending on it, and the slack at all nodes on the path is zero. The first node is not the end of any edge and the last node is not the start of any edge.

During the execution of the operation the nodes represent events in time when all activities incident *to* that node have all been completed and no activities incident *from* it have started. For each node we can calculate the earliest time it can occur, based on the durations of all its predecessors and the latest time it must occur if the operation is not to be delayed, based on the durations of all its successors. The slack at each node is the difference between these two times and a critical path is a path from source to sink along which all nodes have zero slack.

In calculating earliest times, the nodes should be ordered so that for all edges xy in the graph, x must be handled before y. Similarly for latest times, y must be handled before x. This is known as a topological order. It is assumed the nodes are not input in topological order so a sort is necessary.

To perform the topological sort and calculate earliest and latest times we need to know, for each node, its set of predecessors and its set of successors, that is

$$\text{suc}\,(x) = \{y | xy \text{ is an edge in the graph}\} \text{ e.g. suc } (4) = \{3, 6\}$$

and

$$\text{pred}\,(x) = \{y | yx \text{ is an edge in the graph}\} \text{ e.g. pred } (4) = \{2\}$$

The steps in the calculation then are as follows.

(1) Read in the graph data.
(2) Calculate and store suc (x) for all nodes in the graph and check that there is only one first node.
(3) Calculate and store pred (x) for all nodes in the graph and check that there is only one last node.
(4) Perform the topological sort on the nodes and check that the graph is acyclic (that is, no loops occur).
(5) Calculate and store the earliest time for each node.
(6) Calculate and store the latest time for each node.
(7) Calculate the slack for each node.
(8) Find the critical path.
(9) Print the results.

4.9 *Design of a Disc Filing System* The objective of this exercise is to specify the procedures and associated abstract types necessary to provide a simple single user disc filing system. For the purposes of the problem we may consider the filing system to be

    filestore : **array** [1 . . maxnoofiles] **of** file

where a file may be considered to be of type

    record
    attribute : **record**
             filename : identifier;
             size   : 1 . . maxfilesize;
             end
    contents : **array** [1 . . size] **of** page;
    end

and a page is fixed number (such as 256) of words

    type page = **array** [1 . . pagesize] **of** machine word

The number of files currently in use is contained in

    noofiles : 0 . . maxnoofiles

    The essence of the problem is to provide a structure that will allow the filestore to be mapped into the amorphous discpartition set aside to hold the filestore

    discpartition : **array** [1 . . partitionsize] **of** page

For this purpose you are provided with the following primitive operations.

(a)   get (*i* : (1 . . partitionsize); **var** buffer : page; **var** ok : boolean) which transfers (assigns) to buffer the value of the *i*th page of the discpartition and true to ok if the transfer is successful. Buffer is undefined and ok is false if the transfer fails.

(b)   put (*i* : (1 . . partitionsize); buffer : page) which transfers (assigns) to the *i*th page of the discpartition the value of buffer, and true to ok if the transfer is successful. If the transfer fails ok is set false.

The filing system is to provide the following operations.

(a)   noofiles : (0 . . maxnoofiles)
    which returns the number of files currently in existence (initially zero).

(b)   nooffreepages : (0 . . partionsize)
    which returns the number of pages remaining in discpartition that have yet to be allocated to a file.

(c)   create (fileattr : attribute)
    if there is not already a file with name fileattr.filename, and if enough freespace exists in the discpartition, then a new file is added to filestore and noofiles is increased by one. The contents of the new file are undefined.

(d)   erase (filename : identifier)
       if a file with this name exists then it is deleted from filestore and noofiles
       is reduced by one.

(e)   change (fileattr : attribute)
       if there exists a file with fileattr.filename then its size is set to fileattr.size,
       its contents are left undefined.

(f)   open (filename : identifier; mode : (read, write); **var** ok : boolean)
       before the contents of a file can be accessed it must be opened for either
       reading or writing; if the file exists then ok is set true otherwise it is set
       false. A file cannot be open simultaneously for reading and writing.

(g)   close (filename : identifier)
       closing a file makes its contents unavailable for processing until it is next
       opened.

(h)   read (filename : identifier; **var** buffer : page, **var** ok : boolean)
       provides sequential read only accessing to the pages of the file filename.
       The ith call after the file is opened for reading reads the ith page of the file
       contents into buffer. A transfer failure sets ok false otherwise ok is set true

(i)   write (filename : identifier; buffer : page; **var** ok : boolean)
       provides sequential write only accessing to pages of the file filename. The
       ith call after the file is opened for writing writes to the ith page of the file
       contents from the buffer. A transfer failure sets ok false otherwise ok is set
       true.

Your filing system should also perform store management by keeping track of
the discpartition pages as they become allocated and deallocated from files. It
should also be possible to list the attributes of all the files in the filestore (in
alphabetical name order).

4.10 *Design of a Magnetic Tape Filing System* Extend the filing system (exercise
4.4) so that magnetic tape can be handled in a compatible way. In specifying the
primitive operations required by your system, take realistic account of the
handling characteristics of magnetic tape; these factors should also affect the
operations provided by your system.

References

An asterisk indicates the most important references.

Adelson-Velskii, G. M., and Landis, E. M. (1962), *Dok. Akad. Nauk SSSR*, 146, pp. 263–6; English translation in *Soviet Math.*, 3, 1259–63.

Amble, O., and Knuth, D. E. (1974), 'Ordered Hash Tables', *Comput. J.*, 17, 135–42.

Brinch Hansen, Per (1973), *Operating System Principles* (Prentice-Hall, Englewood Cliffs, N.J.).

——— (1975a), 'The Programming Language Concurrent Pascal', *Trans. I.E.E.E. on Software Engineering*, 1, 2.

——— (1975b), 'Concurrent Pascal Report' (Information Science, California Institute of Technology).

——— (1976), 'SOLO Operating System', *Software Practice and Experience*, 6, 141–206 (four papers).

Coleman, D. (1977a), 'The Systematic Design of File-processing Programs', *Software Practice and Experience*, 7, 371–81.

——— (1977b), 'Finite State Machine Theory and Program Design: A Survey', *Computer Studies Quarterly*, 1, to be published.

*Dahl, O. J., Dijkstra, E. W., and Hoare, C. A. R. (1972), *Structured Programming* (Academic Press, London) 1–82.

Dahl, O. J., Myhrhand, B., and Nygaard, K. (1970), 'The SIMULA 67 Common Base Language' (Norwegian Computing Centre, Oslo, Publication No. S-22).

Dijkstra, E. W. (1968), 'Goto Statement Considered Harmful', *Communs Ass. comput. Mach.*, 11, 147–8, 538, 541.

——— (1972), 'Notes on Structured Programming', in O. J. Dahl, E. W. Dijkstra and C. A. R. Hoare, *Structured Programming* (Academic Press, London).

——— (1973), 'Hierarchical Ordering of Sequential Processes', in C. A. R. Hoare and R. H. Perrot (eds), *Operating System Techniques* (Academic Press, London).

——— (1976), *A Discipline of Programming* (Prentice-Hall, Englewood Cliffs, N.J.).

*Gries, D. (1974), 'On Structured Programming – A Reply to Smoliar', *Communs Ass. comput. Mach.*, 17, 655–7.

Griffiths, M. (1975), 'Requirements for and Problems with Intermediate Languages for Programming Language Implementation' (Lecture notes for the NATO International Summer School, Marktoberdorf, W. Germany).

Hetzel, W. C. (1973), *Program Test Methods* (Prentice-Hall, Englewood Cliffs, N.J.).

Hoare, C. A. R. (1962), 'Quicksort', *Comput. J.*, 5, 10–15.

—— (1968), 'Record Handling', in F. Genuys, *Programming Languages* (Academic Press, London) 291–347.

—— (1972a), 'Proof of Connection of Data Representations', *Acta Informatica*, 1, 271–81.

—— *(1972b), 'Notes on Data Structuring', in O. J. Dahl, E. W. Dijkstra and C. A. R. Hoare, *Structured Programming* (Academic Press, London).

—— *(1974), 'Monitors: An Operating System Structuring Concept', *Communs Ass. comput. Mach.*, 17, 549–57.

—— (1975), 'Recursive Data Structures', *Int. J. comput. inf. Sci.*, 4, 105–32.

Hopcraft, J., and Ullman, J. (1969), *Formal Languages and their Relation to Automata* (Addison-Wesley, Reading, Mass.).

Horowitz, E. (1975), *Practical Strategies for Developing Large Software Systems* (Addison-Wesley, Reading, Mass.).

Hoskyns, J. (1973), Implications of Using Modular Programming, Guide No. 1 (John Hoskyns, New York).

Jackson, M. J. (1975), *Principles of Program Design* (Academic Press, London).

Jensen, K., and Wirth, N. (1975), *Pascal: User Manual and Report* (Springer-Verlag, New York).

*Knuth, D. E. (1968), *The Art of Computer Programming, Volume 1 Fundamental Algorithms*, 2nd ed. (Addison-Wesley, Reading, Mass.) chapter 2.

—— (1973), *The Art of Computer Programming, Volume 3 Searching and Sorting* (Addison-Wesley, Reading, Mass.).

—— (1974), 'Structured Programming with Gotos', *Comput. Surv.*, 6, 260–301.

Landin, P. J. (1966), 'The Next 700 Programming Languages', *Communs Ass. comput. Mach.*, 9, 157–66.

Lister, A. M. (1975), *Fundamentals of Operating Systems* (Macmillan, London and Basingstoke).

Madnick, S. E. (1967), 'String Processing Techniques', *Communs Ass. comput. Mach.*, 10, 420–4.

Naur, P. (1969), 'Programming by Action Clusters', *BIT*, 9, 250–63.

Naur, P., and Randell, B. (eds) (1969), 'Software Engineering' (Scientific Affairs Division, NATO, Brussels).

Newell, A., and Tonge, F. (1960), 'An Introduction to Information Processing Language V', *Communs Ass. comput. Mach.*, 3, 205–11.

Peterson, W. W., Kasami, T., and Tokura, N. (1973), 'On the Capabilities of while, repeat and exit Statements', *Communs Ass. comput. Mach.*, 16, 503–12.

Sussenguth, E. H. (1963), 'Use of Tree Structures for Processing Files', *Communs Ass. comput. Mach.*, 6, 272–9.

Warnier, J. D. (1974), *Logical Constuction of Programs* (Stenfert Kroese N.V., Leiden).

Wijngaarden, A. Van (ed.) (1969), 'Report on the Algorithmic Language ALGOL 68', *Num. Math.*, 14, 79–218.

Wilkes, M. V. (1964), 'An Experiment with a Self-compiling Compiler for a Simple List-processing Language', in R. Goodman, *Annual Review in Automatic Programming* (Pergamon, Oxford).

Wirth, N. (1971), 'Program Development by Stepwise Refinement', *Communs. Ass. comput. Mach.*, 14, 221–7.

—— (1973), *Systematic Programming* (Prentice-Hall, Englewood Cliffs, N.J.).

—— (1974), 'On the Composition of Well-structured Programs', *Comput. Surv.*, 6, 247–59.

—— *(1975), *Algorithms + Data Structures = Programs* (Prentice-Hall, Englewood Cliffs, N.J.).

Woodward, P. M., and Jenkins, D. P. (1961), 'Atoms and Lists', *Comput. J.*, 4, 47–53.

Yourdon, E. (1975), *Techniques of Program Structure and Design* (Prentice-Hall, Englewood Cliffs, N.J.).

Index